The Academic Ethic

The Academic Ethic
Edward Shils

The Report of a Study Group
of the International Council on the
Future of the University

Jeanne Hersch, Torsten Husén,
Thomas Nipperdey, John Passmore,
Gerd Roellecke, Edward Shils,
Bruce Smith, Charles Townes

University of Chicago Press
Chicago and London

The University of Chicago Press, Chicago 60637
The University of Chicago Press, Ltd., London

Reprinted from *Minerva*, vol. 20:1–2
© 1983 by *Minerva*
All rights reserved. Published 1983
University of Chicago Press edition 1984
Printed in the United States of America

93 92 91 90 89 88 87 86 85 84   1 2 3 4 5

Library of Congress Cataloging in Publication data

Shils, Edward Albert, 1911–
    The academic ethic.

    "The report of a study group of the International
Council on the Future of the University, Jeanne Hersch . . .
[et al.]"
    Includes bibliographical references.
    1. College teachers—Professional ethics.   I. Inter-
national Council on the Future of the University.
II. Title.
LB1779.S44   1984   174'.9379   84-6
ISBN 0-226-75330-1
ISBN 0-226-75332-8 (pbk.)

Table of Contents

INTRODUCTION

The Academic Ethic has a dual source. In 1969 Sir Eric (now Lord) Ashby delivered an address before the British Academy entitled "The Academic Profession".[1] It was devoted largely to the obligations of university teachers to their students. I was very sympathetic with Eric Ashby's courageous entry into a subject very little discussed in that time when large parts of the student bodies in many countries were creating a deafening uproar. Not many senior academics were inclined to speak calmly and with an eye on what was essential and I did not forget his uniquely dispassionate and earnest effort.[2]

Shortly after the foundation of the International Council on the Future of the University I urged the late Professor Charles Frankel, the founder and chairman of the Council to establish a study-group on the subject of Eric Ashby's lecture. He did so; one meeting, attended by Ashby and Professors Dieter Henrich of Heidelberg University, Raymond Aron of the Collège de France, Charles Townes of the University of California at Berkeley and John Passmore of the Australian National University was held under Charles Frankel's chairmanship. No further meetings were held. I emphasized many times to Charles Frankel that the group should be reconvened but other obligations were more pressing for him. In 1980, Charles Frankel and his wife were murdered in their sleep by two burglars. Piety towards Charles Frankel's memory as well as conviction of the importance of the subject prompted me to keep alive the idea of a study-group on the ethical obligations of the academic profession.

In 1980 with the approval of the board of trustees of the International Council, Professor Thomas Nipperdey of the University of Munich applied successfully to the Thyssen Stiftung for a grant in support of the project entitled "Responsibilities and Ethics of the Teaching Profession: An Investigation of the Academic Ethos". The study-group was accordingly reconstituted with the following membership: Jeanne Hersch, professor emeritus of philosophy, University of Geneva; Torsten Husen, professor of education, University of Stockholm; Thomas Nipperdey; John Passmore; Gerd Roellecke, professor of legal and political philosophy, University of Mannheim; Dr. Bruce Smith, political scientist, Brookings Institution, Washington D.C. and Charles Townes and myself; Professor Nipperdey served as chairman. The group held three meetings. The first meeting of the group was held in Lisbon at the Gulbenkian Foundation in April 1981 in conjunction with the third conference of the International Council; the second was held in October of the same year at the National Humanities Center at Chapel Hill, North Carolina and the third and final meeting in June 1982 at the Werner Reimers-Stiftung in Bad Homburg.

---

[1] "The Academic Profession: Fourth Annual Lecture under the Thank Offering to Britain Fund, 11 June 1969" (London: Oxford University Press for the British Academy, 1969).

[2] I reprinted it in Reports and Documents, *Minerva*, VIII (January 1970) pp. 90–99. It has since been reprinted in Ashby, Eric, *Adapting Universities to a Technological Society* (San Francisco: Jossey-Bass, 1974), pp. 73–87.

2

At the first meeting, topics were enumerated and allocated to members of the group; at the second meeting, the various contributions were presented and discussed. Perhaps because my own contribution was the most voluminous, it fell upon me to write the report; I did this in February 1982. The typescript was circulated to all members of the group and to Joseph Ben-David, professor of sociology, Hebrew University of Jerusalem. The group at its meeting in Bad Homburg presented its comments on the draft. The draft was then revised two more times, bearing in mind the general observations and detailed comments which had been made orally at the Bad Homburg meeting or which were submitted in written form or in annotations on the typescript. This is how the pages which follow came into existence.

The Thyssen Stiftung in its annual report for 1981–82 said "The report is not to be addressed to philosophers but to the academic world as a whole and also to university administrators and to politicians whose decisions affect them. It is concerned not only with old and large universities but it takes into account the great expansion of universities and deals with the situation and the particular tasks of teachers in newly established universities as well."[3]

The Academic Ethic is indeed addressed to the academic profession in all Western countries and to those whose universities have grown up in the traditions of Western universities. The problems of universities are numerous and complex and *The Academic Ethic* does not deal with all of these by any means. It is not presented as an exhaustive analysis of the present situation of universities. It is concerned primarily and above all with the attitudes of university teachers and it asserts and reaffirms their traditional obligations.

No attempt has been made to be original or to be exhaustive. It does not discuss every kind of situation in which the moral attitudes of teachers in their diverse activities can make a difference for good or ill. It is not a code of professional conduct. It is intended rather to arouse reflection and discussion and in so doing to fortify the better dispositions which are already at work in most university teachers, to encourage them in some things and to caution them in others. It is on these fundamental dispositions and on the reflectiveness, the reasonableness and the moral self-consciousness of university teachers that the well-being of universities depends. Without these moral virtues, financial resources and administrative arrangements, although obviously necessary, can never resolve the difficulties and dilemmas of the academic profession and the universities which sustain university teachers in their search for truths of varying degrees of generality and their transmissions of those truths in various forms to their pupils and their fellow-citizens.

E.S.

---

[3] Fritz Thyssen Stiftung, *Jahresbericht 1981/82* (Cologne, 1982), p. 8.

THE ACADEMIC ETHIC

AN INHERENT COMMITMENT

The Task of the University: Universities have a distinctive task. It is the methodical discovery and the teaching of truths about serious and important things. Part of the task is to enhance the students' understanding and to train them in the attitudes and methods of critical assessment and testing of their beliefs so that they can make what they believe as free from error as possible. The discovery and transmission of truth is the distinctive task of the academic profession, just as the care of the health of the patient is the distinctive task of the medical profession, and the protection, within the law, of the client's rights and interests is the distinctive task of the legal profession. The teaching of specific truths postulates a more general affirmation of the value of truth about any specific object or about any general class of objects. That truth has a value in itself, apart from any use to which it is put, is a postulate of the activities of the university. It begins with the assumption that truth is better than error, just as the medical profession accepts that health is better than illness and the legal profession begins with the belief that the assurance of rights under the law is better than to be at the mercy of arbitrary power.

These concepts—truth, knowledge, rights, health—are none of them wholly unambiguous. The doctrine that there is such a thing as truth, that the quest for it is intrinsically valuable has become associated in many academic minds with "metaphysics", "theology", "idealism", "dogma", "religion"—in brief, with all those beliefs and modes of thinking against which many scientists and scholars have rebelled. There is abroad today a desire, more frequently expressed by academics in the humanities and the social sciences, to derogate or even to dissolve the idea that truths can be discovered and taught. Denial of the possibility of detachment, denial of the possibility of the disciplined and disinterested search for knowledge, denial of the possibility of objective knowledge, which is true independently of the passions or desires or "material interests" of the discoverer and transmitter have become more common in recent years in certain influential circles of academics. Some academics preach these denials day in and day out. Their actions, however, almost invariably belie their words. They still believe sufficiently in the possibility of rational argument issuing in truthful conclusions to think that what they say should, on the basis of the rationality of their argument and the evidence which they invoke, persuade their hearers and readers of the truthfulness of their denial of the possibility of truth.

The ascertainment of any truth is a difficult matter; the truth must be re-ascertained incessantly. These truths are changed continuously by new discoveries which may indeed be defined as the revision in the light of new observations and analyses of propositions previously held to be true. For these reasons, there must be elements of tentativeness and readiness to revise in the attitudes towards any truths accepted at present. This readiness to revise is not tantamount to relativism. It does not mean that any proposition is just as true as any other proposition or that the truth of a proposition is dependent on the social position or political orientation of the person asserting or accepting it. It means that the propositions held at any moment are the best that could be achieved by the methods of observation and analysis which are acceptable in scientific and scholarly communities. The acceptance of these propositions, with these qualifications, implies an admission that these particular propositions will not so much be proven to be wrong as that they will be shown to require revision and replacement by propositions sustained by better observations and better interpretations.

It is exactly their concern that their statements, made in their teaching or formulated in their research, should be as true as possible, based on the most methodically gathered and analysed evidence, taking into account the state of knowledge in their own particular fields, that characterises the academic profession. That is what justifies the academic life and the existence of the social institutions, especially the university, which sustain that life. The more specific obligations of the academic as such, as distinct from the obligations he shares with other human beings, all flow from his concern for truths about particular things and for the idea of truth in general. Just as if illness is a myth there is no point in having a medical profession, if rights are a myth there is no point in having lawyers, so if truth, objectivity and rational argument are myths there is no point in teaching and research and no point in taking any particular care in such more specific tasks as making academic appointments, giving expert advice, and so on.

That all their work depends on this assumption is a fact which often disappears from sight when academics are immersed in their specialised research and teaching or are distracted by the demands of public engagement. Unless they are professional philosophers, academics do not spend their time thinking about the nature of truth or its relationship to their activities, any more than doctors daily ask themselves what constitutes health and how it differs from illness. They have specific tasks to perform, specific inquiries to make, specific things to teach; they take these tasks as given and they do not worry themselves about the fundamental principles which underlie their specialised activities.

That is why it is urgent to remind university teachers of what they committed themselves to when they entered upon the academic career. Their passionate desire to aid in the movement towards social equality or justice, and to meet requests and satisfy their own desires to contribute to the practical work of society, sometimes causes academics to forget that the cultivation of truth in all the fields which they study and teach and the respect for truth in their practical activities are essential to and distinctive of their calling. These other social objectives can well exist alongside the methodical search for reliable knowledge in research and its communication in teaching. However, without their primary activity of discovering and teaching the truth as scrupulously and as methodically as they can in the fields for which they are responsible, university teachers would be no more than agitators for social arrangements which they think desirable, or a special sort of leisure class, which is "kept" by society because some of its members, such as the teachers of medicine, law, chemistry, or engineering, perform useful services for society through their own research and their teaching and consultation.

There are, of course, two other views about the function of academics and academic institutions which we do not wish to ignore. We shall, indeed, often advert to them in what follows. The first is that the sole object of universities is to prepare students to fit into particular occupational roles; the second is that the function of universities is to be centres of revolutionary change. About the first view of the task of universities, it should be said that while it is certainly true that universities should, among other things, train students to perform effectively in certain occupations, not every form of training for an occupation is appropriate to universities. Only training for those occupations which rest upon a foundation of fundamental knowledge, as distinct from consisting almost entirely of practical skills, is appropriate for universities. The universities do and ought to educate for those occupations which demand of their practitioners a mastery of a coherent body of organised knowledge, a capacity to assess evidence and a readiness to look at situations afresh. A university education should not have as a task to prepare students for occupations which deal with routine tasks. It should offer education for those occupations which require a knowledge of fundamental processes, principles and methods of analysis. As to the argument that universities should be centres of revolutionary action, it should be emphasized that universities have often been the points or centres of origin of profound changes in the world at large. These have been changes based on an intellectual foundation; many changes in economic and social life have come about in consequence of the intellectual achievements of academic scientists and scholars, for example, in economics, sociology, physics, chemistry and biology. But to think of universities as centres of political agitation is to assign to them a responsibility which properly belongs to political parties, not to universities. Indeed, the suggestion that students and their teachers should together stand for a particular political attitude which they can then impose on the world at large would be comically absurd were it not, in its effects, so tragic. They should stand together for two things: for intellectual integrity and freedom of inquiry. But that is not a political programme, in and of itself, even if it has political implications.

Investigation, and teaching the manner and the results of investigation, are the things that universities know how to do and can do well. It is not more arbitrary to regard them as the function of universities than it is to regard healing as the function of physicians. Some doctors will put money-making or the elevation of their social status or the protection of medical monopolies before healing. But they are then poor physicians. So are those academics poor academics who fail to give primacy to discovery and teaching.

The academic profession is not singled out here for attention because it is worse than other learned professions. Nor are we discussing its ethical problems and obligations because the academic profession was once perfect and has since then fallen dangerously away. As the situation of professions changes, their ethical obligations need reformulation in the face of new tasks. It is not that the fundamental principles change but rather their application to new situations. There is no profession which is exempt from fundamental ethical obligations; there is none which does not constantly encounter conditions causing those ethical obligations cynically to be transgressed or innocently to be overlooked in the concentration of attention on the vigorous pursuit of subsidiary and quite legitimate objectives. There have always been such situations in academic life throughout the whole history of universities. The present situation of universities is one of these but it is also, in some respects, unique. Over the past third of a century, new conditions and new demands on universities have emerged. The world became busier, more things seemed to be happening. Politics became more interesting to more academics as the air filled with wars and rumours of wars, amplified by radio and television-broadcasting. New opportunities for all sorts of extra-academic activities came into existence.

Students became much more numerous, universities became larger and their teaching staffs expanded greatly. Many new universities were founded. More demands were placed on universities. The attention of university teachers was more drawn into the problems of the society which surrounded them. Universities became more dependent on and were more pressed by governments than was the case until the Second World War in liberal-democratic societies. More was demanded of universities and they also became more costly. Universities have become more exposed to public scrutiny than they used to be and many administrators and teachers have sought publicity for themselves and their universities. Universities now have many more administrative officers than they used to have. Universities have become more disaggregated than they used to be.

The past decade has been a period of straitened financial circumstances, of diminished opportunities for the younger generation of scientists and scholars to find appointments, of increasingly complicated relationships of the universities with governments and private business and political organisations. This decade of financial construction has followed a quarter of a century of great expansion and almost euphoric optimism. The disorder both in the student body and in the teaching corps have all left marked traces in the diversion of attention from some of the central tasks of academic life. Many teachers have continued to do their duty, and, of course, great numbers of teachers have applied themselves unreservedly to research. Nevertheless, in recent decades, the sure moral touch has weakened and the self-confidence of the academic profession in its devotion to its calling has faltered. There is a need for the profession to clarify in its own mind and to reaffirm the fundamental obligations inherent in its undertaking.

The present report is intended to contribute to the reanimation of discussion regarding the proper end of academic persons and of academic institutions. Aside from a few fragmentary starts, which have been responses to particular abuses and grievances, the academic profession has done very little to promulgate a set of guiding principles which should govern its custodianship of knowledge in teaching and research, its role in the internal conduct of universities and its participation in the public sphere. Such a set of principles should be broad enough to cover the main fields of activities in which the academic profession engages in its concentration on the acquisition and transmission of knowledge at ever-higher levels of complexity. The principles should apply to all the activities in which academics participate, including not only their scientific, scholarly and pedagogical activities and their conduct within academic institutions but also their publicistic and political activities and their performance of advisory and consultative services for government, private business and political and civic associations.

The obligations of the university teacher are as many-sided as his[1] role. Important though the role of the teacher is, the university teacher is not solely a teacher. Teaching is only one part of the activity of one who is appointed to teach in a modern university. There is an expectation that university teachers should do some research; research is to be regarded, if with differing emphases and in differing proportions, as an obligation of the same order as teaching. Of course, not all teachers will distribute their intellectual energy and interest in the same pattern; some will do mainly teaching and relatively little research, others much more research than teaching. Nor will all universities have the same pattern; some will do much more research than teaching; some will do much more research than others. In those which do little research, it should be accepted as obligatory for those who concentrate mainly on teaching to keep abreast of the most important research for the purposes of their teaching. A university teacher is, furthermore, a member of an academic institution which is more than an administrative facility for his teaching and research; he is a member of a department and of the teaching staff of a university. He is also a member of a scientific and scholarly profession and of an intellectual community which runs beyond the boundaries of his department, his university, his profession and his country. He is also a citizen of his own larger society to which he has, by virtue of his larger and more elaborate stock of rigorously founded knowledge, more than the obligations of the ordinary citizen.

The special obligations of a university teacher derive from his possession of a stock of knowledge such as other persons, who do not devote themselves to the systematic and concentrated acquisition of knowledge, do not possess. The belief that the knowledge an academic possesses is applicable to important practical concerns such as health, economy, military security, industrial production, etc., is a source of deference. The granting of deference to a person in consequence of his possession of special knowledge on important topics is not the result of a deliberate search for deference on the part of the possessor of the knowledge. He does not owe gratitude to those who grant him that deference. What he does owe them is an obligation not to abuse their respect for him.

A body of substantive knowledge in itself has, simply as knowledge, no necessary implications for the conduct of its possessor; yet in certain ways, it does have such implications. It implies above all a concern for the truthfulness of what is asserted as knowledge. It is with this implication that we will be concerned. Knowledge of the various consequences of urbanisation, for example, does not entail any particular course of action. It leaves open the question how these consequences are to be weighed against one another, which is something about which individuals can disagree. But when an academic makes an assertion of these consequences as constituting

---

[1] Wherever "he" or "his" is used to refer to the individual university teacher, both men and women are to be understood.

knowledge, he should do so only if he has done all he could do to ensure that they are indeed the actual consequences. In short, the possession and communication of knowledge implies respect for the rules or methods for the pursuit of knowledge; it entails affirmation of and strict adherence to the criteria of truthfulness as they operate in the particular field or discipline. This in its turn entails modesty in making proposals based, for example, on demographic and sociological studies of problematical validity. And this, in its further turn has implications for the mode of transmission of knowledge, whether it be to young students, to the wider public or to the powerful in society.

The academic ethic is the sum of these obligations which are involved in the pursuit and transmission of advanced knowledge and in roles and in conduct affected by the real or presumed possession of such knowledge. The academic ethic really exists. It is not something excogitated outside the academic realm and offered as an alternative to what goes on there. It is already adhered to by most academics, especially in their research. It is the aspiration of this report to articulate it more explicitly, elaborate some of its implications, and to help colleagues to think about what is entailed ethically in the life and activity of an academic. Conditions have arisen in recent decades in Western societies which have debilitated this ethical commitment. The debilitation must not be exaggerated but it must also be recognised that the present situation is not without its troubling aspects.

The Possession of Advanced, Complex and Reliable Knowledge and its Obligations: University teaching in the present century has been regarded as more than just an occupation through which a livelihood is obtained. When it is called a "profession", it is meant that, in some important way, it differs from other occupations, the fortunes of which are to be determined by the vicissitudes of the market or syndical power or governmental decision. It has been thought to be one of those occupations with special qualities which confer special privileges and obligations on those who practise them. Although in recent years, many occupations have sought to be designated as "professions", a profession still remains what it was thought to be for some centuries, namely an occupation the practice of which requires a more than ordinary amount of complex knowledge, acquired by persistent and systematic study and authoritatively certified. This is true primarily of law, medicine, engineering and the academic profession. The first three are engaged in the practical application of knowledge about particular kinds of situations and objects. The first three of these professions deal with relatively restricted parts of the entire body of systematically studied and acquired knowledge while the academic profession, through its internal division of labour, covers the entire range of systematically studied, methodically gained knowledge parts of which are applied in law, medicine and engineering.

The primary task of the academic profession is the acquisition and transmission of knowledge, not its application. The academic profession receives, assimilates and discovers knowledge by methodical study, and it interprets and transmits that knowledge; it transmits knowledge about the methods of discovery and especially of the validation of knowledge. Even when the teacher's concern is the application of knowledge to practical activities, he himself is not applying the knowledge which he teaches to practical activities. In the teaching of technology, for example, the teacher is transmitting knowledge about the application of knowledge. He teaches how knowledge of a particular substance is applied and can be applied to particular practical tasks. He is not applying that technological knowledge himself. The teacher of engineering in a university is not, in his teaching, performing the practical activities of the engineer. The teaching in a university of the principles and techniques of the application of knowledge in clinical medicine, legal procedure, architectural design and engineering-construction is the transmission of bodies of knowledge and of the rules or methods governing their application. A great deal of university teaching is not about practical application at all; it teaches what is known about particular phenomena and classes of phenomena and how to learn more about them. It tries to dispel error, confusion and misunderstanding.

In modern universities, teaching is associated with research or at the very least, a sustained effort to keep in touch with what is happening in research. The teacher does research and he also bases his teaching on the research done by others and himself, where this bears on the subject of his teaching. Research itself is the methodical acquisition of knowledge, hitherto unknown. Knowledge languishes and fades if it is not cultivated by research. Teaching too languishes if it is not sustained by research. Even though a particular teacher himself does relatively little research, he has to be informed about the research which is being done on his subject. Knowledge is not self-sustaining; it does not grow of itself. It has to be actively sought and brought into teaching to remain alive. These are among the first responsibilities of the academic.

But if they differ in some respects, there is still a major similarity among all the learned professions. Each of them possesses large stocks of complex and advanced knowledge which have not been mastered by the laity of clients, patients and students to whom the learned professions address themselves. This inequality in the possession of knowledge gives to the possessors of knowledge large opportunities to abuse that position of superiority.

The university teachers' possession of more and more intricate knowledge—greater in amount and in intensity, more fundamental and more strictly criticised and tested—than is available to the layman places special obligations on him. These differences in the amount and quality of the knowledge possessed by academics and by laymen are ultimately the ground for the invitation of academics to give "expert" advice to governments and private bodies. Academics are reputed to have not only specialised knowledge and achievement and the habit of objectively considering alternatives; they are reputed to have scholarly, detached and dispassionate judgement. For a variety of reasons, the reputation of the academic profession is at present in danger of discredit.

In the academic profession, the privileges of university autonomy and academic freedom—the very considerable autonomy of decisions in appointment and promotion, in methods of teaching, in the definition of courses of study and of the setting and marking of examinations—as well as the far-reaching freedom of initiation and conduct of scientific and scholarly investigation and the freedom of publication are all, in principle, justified by the greater knowledge possessed by academics in their respective subjects, in comparison with the knowledge possessed by students and laymen. The corporate autonomy of universities rests also on certain legal traditions, which continue a principle of corporate self-government once shared by guilds and estates and which took form prior to the emergence of modern society. The main argument for the autonomy of universities, aside from more general arguments from tradition and for a pluralistic organisation of society, is that the validity of the knowledge which academics teach and discover can be assessed only by those who have mastered it by long and intensive study.

The special privileges of university autonomy and academic freedom are accorded in consequence of the belief of the laity that academics possess knowledge which it appreciates and desires. These privileges in turn engender obligations. The obligations of the academic profession are inherent in the custodianship of the pursuit, acquisition, assessment, and transmission of knowledge through systematic study, in accordance with methodical procedures including observational techniques, rules of evidence and principles of logical reasoning. The obligation to adhere to these norms is entailed in the acceptance of this custodianship. The commitment to rigorous methods of inquiry and of assessment of the results of enquiry is inherent in the decision to pursue an academic career.

A person who enters on an academic career might do so on the ground that it is an easy and quiet life, or that it is reasonably well remunerated, well regarded and likely to place the person who has chosen it in pleasant surroundings. Or he might, while at first being attracted to the academic life for academic reasons, come to have little interest in research and teaching, engaging in them in a humdrum way as one does a job which does not hold one's heart. There are undoubtedly many academics like this who have lost their zeal and who fall short of the standard which they know ought to prevail. Nevertheless, the ethical principle which is implicit in academic activity is not hidden from most of those who have chosen to enter the academic career; it is never far from their consciousness, however far they stray from it. Once their choice has been made, they cannot free themselves from their obligations as academics, even if they do not participate whole-heartedly in the life of teaching and research.

If one engages voluntarily in the activities of teaching and in research, of acquiring, assessing, transmitting and discovering knowledge, one is committed to the acknowledgement of the differences between truth and falsity and to the greater value of the former over the latter. One commits oneself to adherence to the methods which help to distinguish between truth and falsity. One acknowledges that there are criteria outside one's own desires and convenience by which one may distinguish the true from the false; one acknowledges that there are techniques and modes of reasoning which help to distinguish truth from falsity. These include the adduction of evidence, critically assessed, by the use of the criteria of reliability and validity and of the rational comparison of alternative interpretations.

The acceptance of propositions is justifiable by more than a judgement of their convenience or of their practical value; it is justified by a judgement of the validity of the grounds for holding them. It is a judgement that they are more likely to be true and it implies an acceptance of criteria whereby that greater likelihood of truthfulness is arrived at and tested. The prospect that these criteria may become more precise with the passage of time does not absolve anyone from adhering to the criteria, which, at any given time, are as precise as it lies within human powers to make them.

Universities would never have achieved the status which they are accorded in civilised societies if they had not demonstrated that they sought, acquired and presented reliable knowledge. Universities have passed through many vicissitudes and one of the main reasons why, from time to time, their status has declined and responsible parts of their societies have turned against them has been their negligence or indolence in the pursuit of truth by the best-known methods and by the best, currently possible, assessment of received and transmitted knowledge.

THE NEW SITUATION OF UNIVERSITIES AND
ITS CHALLENGE TO THE ACADEMIC ETHIC

The academic ethos has grown out of a long tradition. It has its origins in the time when there were no universities, but only learned men seeking reliable and fundamental knowledge. It goes far back into the long period before the formation of modern science. It was practised by devoted university teachers and by scientists long before it began to appear in very rudimentary formulations in connection with the reform of the German universities in the first decade of the nineteenth century. Even at the height of the glory of the German universities from the last third of that century, when German university professors thought themselves to be almost at the pinnacle of German society, the promulgation of an academic ethic was not taken in hand. Perhaps it was thought to be superfluous. Nor did it appear urgent to academics in the United States, Great Britain and France as the universities in those countries entered into a new phase of creativity. The academic ethic must have seemed self-evident to the academics of the first quarter of the present century. In the United States, where academics came more frequently into conflict with the earthly powers of the state, the press and the economy, much attention was given to the assertion of the rights of academics. Obligations were accepted as self-evident.

Meanwhile, societies were changing and with them the universities were changing too. The obligations which were given in the calling of science and learning have not changed but the conditions in which they are to be brought into action have changed. The universities have become very much larger; more services are demanded of them; their members have become more demanding financially. The universities have been more closely observed by the larger public and they themselves are more aware of this public attention and more desirous of it. All of these changes have affected the morale of the academic profession.

The "Mass University": The "mass university"—the university with more than 20,000 students—is not universal. In Great Britain it does not exist; in the United States many of the leading private universities are smaller. Yet, even short of this arbitrary figure, the universities nearly everywhere have acquired some of the features of mass universities. Mass universities and approximations to them present challenges to the academic ethic which have not been resolved.

The sheer increase in size in both student body and teaching staff has rendered it difficult to maintain the kinds of relations among students and teachers and among colleagues which are necessary for a university to maintain a high morale in its devotion to the advancement of learning through teaching and research. In its more extreme manifestations it has alienated students from the teaching staff and it has isolated many teachers from many of their students. Many individuals in each category are proud of the eminence in science and scholarship which has been attained in the particular mass university with which they are affiliated and of the excellent education and training which they received there. Many of the teachers in mass universities in the United States where the state universities have been large for a long time, are proudly attached to their universities through their pride in the achievements of their most eminent colleagues; they are also sustained in that attachment by their simultaneous membership in the larger academic and scientific communities which transcend the boundaries of any single university and which have their branches or sections in parts of many universities.

This experience of intense intellectual activity and high achievement in some teachers and students at some of these mass universities casts a light, which is both awakening and deceptive, over the mass universities. It has been an awakening light to some of those who have come into contact with it and who have been quickened by it into an intellectual curiosity and exertion which they did not know before and which they might not have reached had it not been for their contact with those persons in the teaching staffs and student bodies who have been the bearers in those mass universities of the scientific and academic ethic.

It is also a deceptive light because it has covered and transfigured to the larger society the rest of the university on which it shines. It has obscured the laxity in standards of teaching, the listlessness of many of the students and the perfunctoriness of their performance in the university.

Even in universities in which the academic and scientific ethos were at the highest level and which were relatively small, there were many time-servers and shirkers or persons whose talents and exertions did not measure up to a high standard. The most famous German universities in their greatest days had a sizeable proportion of members who did little that was significant in teaching and research. It is true that there have always been blank and dreary spots in teaching—if there had not been, there would not be such pleasure in recalling "famous teachers". It is also true that in the Continental universities, which did not share in the tradition of the principle of *in loco parentis*, the professors took little interest in their students except for the very outstanding ones. The seminars however did permit a closer intellectual contact with students who showed promise of becoming scholars or scientists. This has now become more difficult with the increased size of seminars.

One of the things repugnant to the academic ethic which has happened in the mass universities, especially in the United States and the Federal German Republic is that many of the students in the humanities and the social sciences have been abandoned by their teachers to the domain of the unreclaimable. This has not been an explicit decision; it has become part of the culture of mass universities in a number of countries; it has become a part of what is taken for granted. It is based on a conviction that the capacities of the students are weak and that they cannot master an exacting syllabus. They are assigned intellectually shabby text books and thin reading lists. In the mass universities of the United States, they are consigned in many places and subjects to junior teachers who because they teach the lower years feel that they have been cast into a lowly status, teaching according to a syllabus which they did not design themselves. The junior teachers themselves tend to be neglected by those above them.

The mass university increased the proportion of the area covered by the blank and dreary patches. The mass universities have grown too greatly and too rapidly in the size of their teaching staffs for the supply in sufficient numbers of teachers of outstanding talents, discipline and devotion to their calling. Furthermore, teaching large classes of uninterested students has a discouraging effect on teachers. Uninterested teachers bore their students. The very large numbers of undergraduates and graduate students have made it difficult for the intellectually most aspiring and most talented students to find their way to teachers who should guide them and who should respond to their intellectual gifts and potentialities; there are of course some teachers in mass universities who seek out such exceptional students; in some cases, special provision is made for exceptional students, as in undergraduate "honours programmes".

In the period of great expansion, a euphoric attitude about the prospects of universities led paradoxically to negligence about the criteria of appointment, especially about the criteria of teaching ability and interest. This negligence contributed to the appointment of indifferent teachers. The size of the newly appointed teaching staffs of universities and, even more important, the large proportion of such newly appointed teachers in many departments have made it difficult for younger teachers to become adequately assimilated into the academic and scientific ethos which some of the older teachers practised.

The mass universities are not only much larger than all but the very largest universities used to be but they have also larger numbers of students who, although they have met all the formal qualifications for admission, are not well qualified for studies at the level of a university. Changes in the syllabuses of secondary schools have resulted in many of their graduates not having the knowledge which earlier in the century was regarded as prerequisite for work at a university. This creates difficulties for teachers as well as for the students. Teachers must teach at a lower intellectual level than they like or they teach "above the heads" of their students. The students are bored or made miserable and as a result "drop out" or prolong their studies over too many years.

Some of the problems of the mass universities had also been problems of the "élite universities" of 50 or 75 years ago but they are now vastly exacerbated. There were undoubtedly persons holding permanent appointments in such universities who were not pleased with the academic career and who fell short of its standards; there were some who flouted the standards of the academic profession, who neglected their teaching and their students, who did little research and who did it with little interest or conviction and who did not care about their institutions. These problems have become more severe as a result of the relatively rapid growth of the mass university.

The mass universities are here to stay for the foreseeable future and the academic ethic must be practised by the teachers of the mass universities as well as by those in universities with smaller student bodies and smaller teaching staffs. Indeed, emphasis on the academic ethic is even more necessary for the present-day mass universities than it was in the smaller outstanding universities of the past century and a half. In the latter, it was more readily assimilated and did not need to be explicitly stated. There was really little need to discuss the academic ethic in the German university of the 1890s or in Oxford and Cambridge in the first half of the present century or in the leading American universities in their best years between the two world wars. Even at that time, there were universities which were little or no better in their respect for the academic ethic than are today's mass universities but since the numbers of students they educated were smaller than they are now, their influence in their respective national higher educational systems was less pronounced.

Some departments in some of the larger universities have become so large that senior teachers do not know their juniors, even by name and face. Something like this has happened in the smaller universities too; in these, senior members might know their younger departmental colleagues but they are ignorant of the younger members of adjacent departments. This is injurious to the assimilation of the younger generation of teachers and to the internal solidarity of the teaching staff as a whole and to their attachment to the university. The teaching staffs of departments with closely connected subject-matters have become more separate from each other. The increase in the size of universities and their constituent faculties and departments has also increased the spatial separation of departments and disciplines from each other; they have increasingly been housed in separate buildings so that their members seldom meet each other. This spatial separation of faculties was always more common in Continental universities, less so in American and British universities. The separation has now been aggravated in both the Continental and the Anglo-American universities.

It might be said these are merely ecological matters and that they have nothing to do with what the universities have as their concern, namely, intellectual things. It should also be said that spatial separation is not new; universities which do not have a single campus have experienced it for a long time. Nevertheless, the increased size of the universities both in numbers of students and in numbers of teachers has accentuated this condition. Furthermore, spatial and social separations do affect intellectual matters. Universities became what they were in their great days because they helped to bring intellectual traditions into focus and concentrated them on individuals by bringing persons of intellectual talent and disposition into contact with each other. The universities enabled them to find each other and to benefit from each other's stimulating and disciplining presence. Their mutual presence—of teachers with teachers, teachers with students and students with students—had the effect of making them more inclined to exert themselves and to stretch their capacities. One deficiency of the mass university is the isolation of the intellectually serious, highly talented student who has the capacity to become a productive scientist or scholar. This kind of student, under present circumstances, is frequently left to himself until fairly late in his career as a student, when he has a better chance of finding a mentor who can help him. This isolation obtains not only among students, between students and teachers but also between teachers and teachers. The academic ethic and the scientific ethic are both inculcated through face-to-face contact and they are maintained at a high level of intensity by such face-to-face contact. Mutual isolation reduces the pressure generated by the presence of other lively, curious and actually and potentially productive minds. The present-day mass university makes this process of the mutual discovery of talented and interested intellectuals more difficult and it thereby hampers—although it certainly does not prevent—the intensification of intellectual exertion.

The constraints of the mass university are exacerbated in the "reformed" mass university of the Continent where malformations consequent on rapid growth to very large size and the ill-considered responses to those malformations have been petrified into law. The *Gruppenuniversität* in Germany and the "democratised" universities of France, the Netherlands and the Scandinavian countries have made the rehabilitation of the academic ethos more difficult because they have aggravated conflict, withdrawal and bureaucratisation. The reforms have denied the postulate of the academic ethic; they have denied that there can be consensus and solidarity about common aims in the university and that the university can be a community devoted to intellectual things, despite the divisions of age, function, status and specialisation. As a result of these spuriously "democratic" reforms, many teachers who would have liked it to be otherwise have withdrawn into their own scientific and scholarly research with a few of their more intellectually advanced students and left the rest to the political factions which have been given constitutional status and official resources. Others work under discouraging conditions, separated from their students by the impersonality of large classes and by the distrust, which is intermittently given a dramatic and disruptive expression by a minority of radical students. Efforts to provide for the future of higher education in science and scholarship by discovering at an earlier stage the more talented students who wish to make academic careers and by trying to help them by drawing them out of their isolation are resisted by the "anti-élitist" pretensions of the present period.

The mass university has been criticised for bringing into itself many young persons who have little intellectual interest. This may be true but it does after all teach many of these young persons the specialised technical knowledge which will be necessary for the practice of their occupations and which are sufficiently desired by society to support that kind of education and to pay for the service of those persons after they graduate.

It is, however, not only the small number of highly talented students who are often overlooked in the mass universities; the much more numerous, less distinguished ones also suffer from neglect. They are given an education which is often little more than a simulacrum of a university education. They, like the better students, are usually taught in large classes and receive little attention from senior teachers. Syllabuses have been allowed to run down in the belief that the ordinary students cannot measure up to a higher standard of performance or that they will balk if too much work is required of them. The university teacher's idea of his obligation to these students tends to become pale and blurred. Many teachers working under these conditions, especially those who are zealous in research, come to regard their teaching of undergraduates as of secondary importance. This is not so true of their attitude towards their own group of research students or of the handful of brilliant undergraduates whom they discover by deliberately searching for them or who deliberately seek them out. They have tended to think of these students as prospective scientists and scholars and their association with them is regarded as closely connected with their own research. The teaching of the other students is often regarded as a chore. This does not always happen; famous scholars and scientists sometimes teach the introductory course in their respective fields but the pleasure in the delivery of polished lectures to large numbers of students does not extend to a sense of obligation to deal with the mass of these ordinary students in smaller groups.

It has always been an issue as to whether academics of outstanding scholarly ability should devote as much time as is done by teachers in Oxford and Cambridge colleges to students of mediocre talent. This question need not be decided here. What is clear, however, is that for a variety of reasons in the mass university many teachers look with some revulsion on teaching large numbers of students of whom they know nothing, whose faces they forget or do not notice and whose names they never know.

One could go on multiplying this list of obstacles which the "reformed" and "democratised" Western European mass university and the mass universities of North America have thrown up in the way of the academic ethic but enough has been said to make clear the magnitude of the task and the urgency of rescuing what can be rescued.

The Service-University: Universities have always been integrated into the practical life of their societies. They have always included among their functions the training of lawyers and physicians; later, they introduced courses for civil servants and advanced secondary school teachers as well, and later still, courses for engineers and scientists who worked in government, agriculture and industry. In the present century, they have continued to do all these things as well as to educate their own succession in science and scholarship and the practitioners of many occupations, such as journalism, librarianship and social work, which did not exist in their present form until quite recently; nursing education has also become in some places a responsibility accepted by universities. For quite a long time in American and British universities, they have also provided training for the management of private business firms.

Despite these perfectly obvious facts, the charge that universities are ivory towers has been a common one throughout the present century. The charge has been made by narrow-minded political zealots who resented the studious detachment of universities in the pursuit of truth in numerous fields of intellectual work and the training of their students to face the facts of life, without dogmatism or rigid prejudice and to apply the best established knowledge in their professional careers. It has also been made by social reformers and radicals who thought that their causes—sometimes good causes, sometimes pernicious ones—could not wait any longer for their realisation, and who required that everyone throw himself into the battle without regard for balanced judgement based on carefully assessed knowledge. Similar criticism of universities used to be made from the quite different standpoint of the "practical man", usually the businessman, who could not see the point of intellectual activities which did not show a profit or which did not contribute directly to industrial and agricultural production.

The criticism of the university as an "ivory tower" has greatly diminished in recent years. Both businessmen and humanitarian reformers, both civil servants and politicians have accepted that the university is not in fact an "ivory tower".

Similarly the universities have practically ceased to be criticised for being too "utilitarian". This was a common view especially in the United States in the early part of this century but such criticism has nearly disappeared. The universities are now regarded by academics, both in principle and by their own individual engagement in practical activities as rightly serving the intellectual–practical demands of their societies. There is a general consensus inside and outside the universities that they should be and are involved in the practical concerns of their societies in so far as these activities have a substantial intellectual—above all scientific—content.

Universities are now regarded as indispensable to more practical activities than were ever conceived before as requiring systematic knowledge, and hence, higher education for the acquisition of that knowledge. There is general agreement about this between most academics on the one hand and the leaders in practical affairs on the other. Local and state governments and national governments in almost all Western countries, private business firms and civic organisations now think that the knowledge which universities produce is necessary to them. They do not think that it is sufficient for them just to appoint the graduates of universities who have had these necessary kinds of fundamental knowledge imparted to them as students before taking up their appointments and who have learned at universities how to acquire the fresh knowledge which their tasks will require.

The prospective "users" of the knowledge and of the techniques of gaining new knowledge which their employees have acquired in universities have however begun to demand something more immediately practical. The first steps were taken about a century and a half ago when enterprisers in chemical industries began to solicit individual academic chemists to do research on problems which were of practical importance to the chemical industry. They began to invite academics to do research designed for immediate practical use, alongside or instead of concentrating on the advancement of fundamental knowledge. More recently they have wanted universities to offer special training courses for already employed persons in order to provide them with very particular kinds of knowledge which have been created since those persons had been trained as regular students. Academics, for their part, began to offer advisory services to help governments or business enterprises to deal with highly specific current problems. These expectations and the positive responses of academics became very common after the Second World War.

Also after the Second World War governments became persuaded that the well-being of their societies, or of particular parts of their societies, would in the future depend on having sufficient numbers of persons with the necessary higher educational qualifications; the "planning of high-level manpower" in one form or another was widely recommended and taken seriously. The universities came to be regarded more specifically than ever before as the places where immediately usable scientific research was and could be performed and where the scientists and other persons could acquire the scientific and technological knowledge which was to be immediately applied in the technology and management of the affairs of industrial and commercial firms and governments. This belief was one of the major reasons for the greatly increased financial support for universities. Although this was not a sharp disjunction from what had been developing over the preceding century, the specificity and insistence of the demands for these practical services in research and education have become much more prominent elements in the conception of the tasks of the university.

This pressure on the universities for the provision of specific "services" in research and training has not been exerted solely by the immediate "users" of these services; nor have the "services" been devised and "pushed" by the universities although the universities have responded very energetically to the new possibilities. Some of the pressure has come from agencies of propaganda like the Organization for Economic Cooperation and Development (OECD) and organs of the United Nations as well as from many foundations, associations, publications and individual publicists arguing for making the universities more "relevant". A large volume of popular writing in books and periodicals about universities was produced after the end of the Second World War. Much of this literature contended that universities must "serve the interests of society" much more directly and deliberately than they had done before. This literature, when combined with the demands made and opportunities offered by governmental and civic bodies, philanthropic foundations and private firms, generated a wave of belief which carried many university teachers and administrators with it.

When in more recent years in the United States, the federal government became more active than it had ever been before in attempting to overcome the disabilities of certain sections of American society, it used its financial power over the universities to make them become its instrument for that egalitarian objective. Teaching hospitals in the poorer sections of large cities which were parts of the institutional system of medical education found themselves becoming "community hospitals" as well. The resources of universities located in large cities were pressed into the provision for groups in their vicinity of certain social services although the beneficiaries of these calls on the revenue of the universities were in no sense members of the universities. This has gone far beyond activities of the "settlement movement" which flourished in British and American universities from the 1880s onward.

The universities perform non-academic services not only for bodies outside the university but for groups inside the university as well. Anglo-American universities traditionally took quasi-parental responsibilities for their students; much of this was informal. Latterly, universities have assumed many additional functions for the welfare of their students and teaching staffs alongside the traditional functions of record-keeping, examining, financial procurement, etc. As they have become larger, and as the number of students having no direct contact with their teachers has increased, specialised offices of advisers and counsellors who are not teachers have also become more numerous. Medical, dental and mental health services for students and staffs became fuller. "Child day-care" centres for the offspring of students and academic and auxiliary staff have in varying degrees been taken on by universities in a number of countries. Similarly, the provision of entertainment and cultural performances for members of the university and the larger public have appeared among the new services of universities, going beyond the provision of athletic spectacles, which was practically unique to American universities and of dramatic and musical performances by students. In all these and other ways, universities have acquired a number of functions which they never had previously. Whatever their moral, social and economic desirability, these activities all increase the size of the administrative staffs of the universities; they bring into the universities a larger number of persons who have no primary interest in intellectual matters and who in the course of time possess vested interests in their own activities and offices. When the financial resources available to the universities are reduced or cease to grow, these non-academic activities, including those which bring no revenue to the universities but which entail only costs as well as those which are associated with the acquisition of revenue, such as "offices of research contracts", are very strong claimants for their share of the budget of the university.

It is not that all these services are useless or despicable. Some of them are outgrowths of the success of the universities in scientific research and in professional training; they are results of the prestige won by the universities through these successes. Many of these services are valuable to society and to the members of the university. Some of them bring revenue to the university which provides them. Nevertheless, they extend the non-intellectual preoccupations of the university and they are distractions from its central responsibilities for teaching and discovery.

The Political University: In the past, churches and governments demanded the faith and loyalty of university teachers. Over the past century and a half and especially in the past half century, the churches have largely abandoned their demand for the faith of the teachers in the diminishing part of the university world which they controlled. In some countries, governments took the loyalty of the teachers for granted; in others loyalty was required of university teachers as persons with the legal status of civil servants. In countries as different as the German Empire and the United States, this loyalty was assured by the dismissal of teachers who were charged with sympathy with or participation in subversive activities or who were affiliated with organisations with allegedly subversive goals; it was also assured by the refusal to appoint persons suspected of such activities or opinions. In wartime, university teachers usually served their governments in various ways as members of the armed forces, as scientific research workers, as administrators and as intelligence officers. Apart from rare instances—more frequent in some countries than in others—university teachers were assumed to be loyal to the existing social order even when some of them were in sharply expressed opposition to it. Revolutionaries also believed that university teachers were loyal to the existing order and they expected no help from the universities in their conflict with it.

The university as an institution was generally accepted as part of the "establishment", *i.e.*, the constellation of the major churches, the leading newspapers, the government itself and the economic leadership of the country. Except for occasional ceremonial affirmation of loyalty and in war-time, the highest officials of the universities, such as presidents, rectors and vice-chancellors, acting on behalf of the universities as institutions asserted no corporate position on political issues. As institutions, universities espoused no partisan attitudes, whatever the attitudes of their individual members. By and large, this situation still obtains and universities have generally been able to avoid being drawn into political controversies in which they would have to declare a position as a party to the controversy. They have on occasion, but not frequently, issued corporate and joint declarations regarding academic freedom or regarding governmental policies in the financial support for universities; associations of vice-chancellors or presidents have sometimes issued statements to inform the public regarding the financial problems of the universities in their respective countries.

In more recent years, this has begun to change. For example, a few years ago, certain leading American universities, acting in their corporate capacity, have declared themselves as *amicae curiae* in controversies regarding "affirmative action" in universities other than their own. This was an unusual step but it was in tune with the spirit of the times. Much more often there have been demands made by students and by members of academic staffs of American universities that their universities, in their corporate capacity, should make public declarations expressing the attitude of the university as a whole denouncing the war in South East Asia in the 1960s and 1970s or about the policies of racial segregation of the South African government. Both radical students and some university professors and presidents have declared that the university should become a "critical university". By this, they have meant, among other things, that a university, as a corporate body, should, through its officially appointed representatives, make public declarations on all kinds of public issues about which some of its members have strong feelings and convictions, regardless of whether these issues touch directly on the university as an institution of teaching and research. Another related demand has been that the university should train their students to develop and express critical attitudes towards the existing social and political order. A small number of radical teachers have in a moment of enthusiastic fantasy tried to turn the precincts or buildings of their universities into asylums for evaders of conscription, terrorists sought by the police, etc.

These demands have on the whole been unsuccessful, although university presidents have since the late 1960s become increasingly disposed individually or collectively to make public declarations on political issues. Another related phenomenon has been the increased frequency over the past several decades with which university teachers have been signatories of partisan "open letters" about political issues to which not only their own names but the names of their universities have been attached. (There has been an increasingly critical attitude towards the attachment of the names of the universities but the practice has continued unchecked.)

Underlying these particular developments has been a heightening of political interest within the academic profession as a whole and particularly in the social science and humanistic faculties. University teachers have long been interested in political issues and a small number of them, in France in the nineteenth century, entered upon political careers. This animation of political interest within the academic profession has been rather pronounced since the agitation about the case of Captain Dreyfus in the last decade of the nineteenth century. In Italy, the United States, and Germany and to a lesser extent in Great Britain, academic social scientists played a significant part in public discussions on political questions and they seem to have had some influence on public opinion. The period since the Second World War has seen a considerable expansion of this kind of activity and an intensification as well. It is against this background that the high degree of sensitivity and the increased force of expression about political matters on such matters as the war in South East Asia, the control of armaments and the developments in formerly colonial territories are to be seen.

University students in liberal-democratic countries have intermittently been drawn into political activities. They have been more inclined towards extreme positions than have their politically interested teachers and their politics have been more demonstrative. The political activities of students in the 1960s and 1970s were probably more fervent and more extensive than ever before and the politically active students made more political demands on their teachers. They also concerned themselves more with the substance of their course of study and with the internal administration and academic appointments in their universities than they had in the past.

One manifestation of the vigour of political partisanship in the universities has been the movement in the social sciences and in the humanities to make appointments with fairly explicit references to political criteria. The view that a department should have representation of "the Marxist view" or "the radical view" is put forward not infrequently by senior members of university departments or of appointive committees who themselves are not Marxists, or it is put forward by members of the department or of the appointments committee who are sympathetic with the radical political standpoint which they wish represented. It is explicitly argued that the Marxist or the radical viewpoint is scientifically distinctive, that it represents an intellectually legitimate approach and that the "pluralism of standpoints"—meaning, in fact, certain particular political standpoints although not usually so explicitly stated—requires the appointment of a Marxist. This argument is apparently seldom adduced when the appointment of non-Marxists is being discussed.

The foregoing observations do not imply that university teachers should be indifferent to the political problems of their societies or of the world at large and they do not imply either that they do not have the same political rights as other citizens. They do point, however, to a phenomenon which can distract academics from their responsibilities for teaching and research in accordance with the best methods available for ascertaining what is true regarding any of the particular subjects and problems they deal with. Among the consequences of politicisation is the appearance of a current of academic opinion which asserts that such truths are not ascertainable by these methods, that all intellectual activity is political by its nature, and that the aspiration for detachment and objectivity is vain and illusory. This opinion hits at the very heart of the academic ethic.

The Governmentally Dominated University: In many liberal-democratic countries, universities were founded on governmental initiative, have depended on the financial support of governments, have had their charters authorised by governments and even had their constitutions and statutes promulgated and enacted by governments. In the Anglo-Saxon countries, governments nearly always issued the charters of universities which permitted them to exist legally as corporate bodies, to own property, etc. In the United States, first in the southern and middle western and then in the western states, the state governments founded universities and supplied the funds for their support. Alongside these there were many private universities which had no financial support from governments. Being supported by government did not mean that the universities were simply instruments of governmental desires and decisions. Governmental financial support was quite compatible with far-reaching autonomy of the universities in Germany as well as in Great Britain and the United States.

Apart from those countries and states in which a secondary school diploma or certificate automatically entitled its holder to have a place as a student in a state university, universities were generally free to set the conditions of admission; except for state-examinations, the setting and marking of examinations were entirely in the hands of the teaching staff of universities. Universities generally appointed members of their teaching staffs and promoted or discontinued them, if they had not been appointed on permanent tenure. They decided what was to be the content of the various courses of study, although they had to bear in mind the requirements for admission to and practice of the various professions for which the university offered training. Professors decided what research should be done in their university-institutes or departments.

Governments generally did not attempt to influence the choice of subjects which students might make, nor did they attempt to influence the proportion which "major" subjects made up in all the subjects studied by the students. When governmental approval of proposals for appointment had to be obtained, it was mainly granted as a matter of course within the list of candidates submitted by the faculty, or the universities were asked to submit an alternative list of proposed candidates. Direct governmental appointments were relatively rare. Universities were entirely free to decide who should be granted degrees and what classes of degrees were to be awarded to students on the basis of their performance on examinations, in research or in their performance in the class-room or in seminars.

Universities have had to move on an intricate pathway in their relations with churches and governments to establish and maintain university autonomy and academic freedom. The paths varied from country to country. Still, by and large, both the autonomy of the university and academic freedom did become established. In at least one country—Germany—academic freedom in teaching and research came to be guaranteed by the constitution. In other countries, it was achieved through conventions which were generally observed even though they did not have the force of law.

With the coming of totalitarianism, this pattern, which was mainly a creation of the second half of the nineteenth century, underwent drastic modification. In the totalitarian countries teachers were appointed on political grounds; other teachers were dismissed on political, ethnic and religious grounds. Admissions of students and the contents of courses of study were regulated according to political criteria. Academic freedom in the sense of freedom to do academic things, *e.g.*, to choose what to teach and how it was to be taught, was far-reachingly curtailed; the civil freedom of academics was of course abolished with that of all other citizens. Universities became infiltrated with academics who, whatever their past performance, became agents of the ruling party. Certain subjects in the natural sciences and humanistic subjects, which were relatively remote from the doctrines espoused by the monopolistic party, continued to exist in a shrunken and obscure condition. Disciplines on which the party's doctrines touched or on which the leaders of the party had views were utterly distorted.

Nothing at all close to this has occurred in the universities of liberal-democratic countries. Nevertheless, governments in such countries, too, have greatly enlarged their interest in and influence over universities. The interest and influence of governments were expressed and intensified by their unprecedentedly large expenditures on universities. The immense expenditures were in fact an expression of their confidence that the universities could, if appropriately provided for and conducted, meet the "needs of society" on behalf of which governments spoke.

Governments have never been completely indifferent to universities, even in Great Britain, where no universities had been governmental institutions except in the sense that they received charters from governments and in the sense that in the provinces and Scotland representatives of local governments sat on the highest governing bodies of the universities. The central government of Great Britain on a number of occasions appointed royal commissions to enquire into the conduct of universities. In the United States, private universities had no connections with governments except for the receipt of a charter from a state government; others were supported by but not closely supervised or regulated by state and municipal governments and they had practically no connections with the central government. In France, Spain and Italy, universities were dependent on the central government for their budget, appointments, the setting of syllabuses, etc. In Germany, universities were legally institutions of the state which provided practically all of their funds, authorised the appointment of their teachers and drew up their constitutions or statutes. Nevertheless, these varying arrangements did not entail very close and continuous surveillance of teaching and research. Most of the universities of liberal-democratic and more or less liberal, monarchical countries enjoyed a considerable degree of autonomy, some by law and some *de facto*. Nevertheless, this autonomy has not made the universities immune from the consequences of variations in governmental policies regarding education and scientific research.

Without requiring any change in standards of admission, governments have greatly influenced the size of the university student bodies. They have done so by promoting the completion of courses of study in secondary schools, which has, in turn, resulted in more young persons acquiring the qualifications for admission to universities; to this, governments have added the provision of grants or loans to pay for fees and maintenance and of grants for the construction of new buildings at universities and for the payment of the salaries of larger teaching staffs. This movement towards the "mass university" has not been a result of direct command by governments to the universities nor has it been entirely a product of governmental policies—there has, in fact, been a tremendous surge of belief throughout Western societies in the desirability and necessity of becoming "educated". The universities themselves welcomed the governmental policies which expanded the size of the student bodies, increased the numbers of universities, etc. The many-sided expansion of the universities owes a great deal to governmental policies. Likewise, the policies have produced the present embarrassments of universities which enlarged their plant and equipment and their teaching staffs on the assumption that governments would continue to provide, because, in recent years, governmentally supplied financial resources have been contracting more than student bodies and teaching staffs and the costs of operation. The contraction or stabilisation of the appropriations made to universities both for the support of students and the support of research have caused many difficulties for universities which had enlarged their staffs and their facilities during the period of expanding financial resources. (Quite recently, the British government has imposed a reduction in the number of students.)

Furthermore, once central governments began to spend huge sums of money on universities and particularly for research in universities, they also became insistent that their money be properly spent. "Accountability" has become a governmental concern which affects universities as recipients of governmental funds. This has been thought to require much closer surveillance over universities. Their expenditures have been more closely watched; the ratio between teachers and students has likewise been more closely watched in a number of countries and the teachers' use of their time has also been questioned as never before. Although there have been efforts by governments to influence the distribution of students among different fields of study, the substance of what is taught has been left untouched. By and large, however, the specifically academic freedom and the civil freedom of university teachers have scarcely ever been greater in the history of universities, as far as intervention and restriction by governments are concerned. Nevertheless, governments have moved nearer to the heart of the university. For one thing, the new system, now nearly half a century old, of the support of research in universities by central governments has made universities more dependent not just for funds—in Continental universities, they were already very dependent on central governments for the financial support of research at a time when universities in English-speaking countries were still largely independent of such support—but on the decisions of governmental officials as to which fields of research would be supported. Governments, spending so much money on research and attributing so much importance to it, have "science-policies"; they have succeeded in doing so with very varying degrees of efficacy and coherence. These science-policies are much influenced by the advice given by academic scientists. Nevertheless, general decisions regarding the allocation of funds among the different fields and groups of problems in which academic scientists work are now being influenced by governments in a greater measure than was the case before the First World War or between the two world wars.

This dependence has by no means been a totally external imposition against the will of academics. In this recent development, the advice of academic scientists has been sought regarding which particular proposals for research should be supported and it has normally been heeded; still, the decision has remained the decision of government officials who at the moment of decision are neither scientists nor university teachers. In decisions about the allocation of funds among the main fields of scientific research, *e.g.*, between astronomy and nuclear physics, the decisions have been made by politicians in cabinets and legislatures and by high civil servants; here too, however, the decisions have usually been made after hearing the views of scientists in various capacities as scientific advisers, university administrators and officials of academies and learned societies.

This shift towards government of the centre of gravity in the making of decisions about the choice of problems for research is much more pronounced in the kinds of governmental research designated as "mission-oriented". While much of this research is done in governmental laboratories, in research institutes which are more or less governmentally supported, and in the laboratories of private business firms which work on contractual terms for governments, a considerable proportion of it is also done in universities on grants and contracts. The decisions as to which of the problems of mission-oriented research should be investigated, are made by governmental officials. It is true that academic scientists, in the countries in which the universities do mission-oriented work, are not compelled to work on these problems and there are indeed many who do not work in mission-oriented research and who are able to obtain funds from other sources which permit them to work on problems of greater interest to themselves. There are, however, many who are content to work on interesting problems set by "outsiders" and for whom the contracts are important because they are enabled thereby to support graduate students or post-doctoral fellows whose scientific careers are dependent on the income which these contracts bring. A great deal of very important work is undoubtedly done in mission-oriented research and it could not have been done without the large sums made available by governments. The fact remains, however, that the increased prominence of mission-oriented research in universities is tantamount to the displacement of the power of decision from within the universities to governments.

American universities have been more directly affected by governmental actions in matters of appointment in ways which have gone far beyond the traditional Continental practice of the requirement of ministerial approval for the creation of new professorial chairs and for the appointments of particular candidates.

In the United States, the federal government for some years has threatened—it still does so—universities with suspension of the financial support of research or funds for the payment of tuition fees if they do not appoint Negroes, women, Mexican-Americans and Puerto Ricans in sufficient numbers. Nothing like this has happened in other liberal-democratic countries. The Continental universities have been subjected in a different way to a far more comprehensive intrusion of governmental authority into their internal affairs. This has occurred through the legislation of the past two decades which has transformed the system of internal government of universities and severely affected their intellectual level and the policies of universities regarding the appointment of university teachers. By transferring much of the power to make decisions regarding the substantive content of syllabuses and courses of study and in some cases, the appointive power as well, to teachers in lower ranks, students and administrative and custodial employees, many European governments have intervened into the internal affairs of universities more penetratingly than has ever happened in liberal-democratic countries. They have done all this while nominally maintaining the academic freedom and the autonomy of universities which in the past were justified by the argument that they guaranteed the predominance of intellectual criteria in the making of decisions about the most important elements of academic life. It is true that the governments of continental countries have over the past century and three quarters at least, had the legal right to frame the constitutions and statutes of universities. Nevertheless, except for the period of National Socialism in Germany, these powers have never been used before to subvert so crucially and systematically the predominance of intellectual academic criteria in the making of decisions on academic matters.

The arrangements vary from one Continental country to another with respect to the composition and powers of governing bodies but whatever their composition, the governmentally guaranteed autonomy of the university from government means that "interest groups" within the university are encouraged to contend for their "interests". These are often political and economic interests.

The Bureaucratised University: The growth in size of the university in numbers of students and teachers, the greatly increased sums of money involved in the operation of a university, the increased intensity and complexity of relations with government, the increased provision of services by the university and the reluctance of university teachers to take responsibilities for activities beyond their own research and teaching has brought about a situation of increased bureaucratisation in the administration of universities. Max Weber made the bureaucratisation of the university one of the main themes of his analysis of science and scholarship as a vocation. He compared the new conditions with the situation which had obtained in the early part of the nineteenth century when professors still worked in their own private libraries and used their own premises and equipment. He remarked on the bureaucratisation of the university as one aspect of the bureaucratisation which had been going on in many spheres of society during his own lifetime. "Self-administration" was one of the characteristic features of the German universities. Except for the *Kurator*, who was the representative of the state government in the university, all higher administrative posts in Continental universities were filled by academics for short periods after which they returned to their regular academic duties. The ancient universities of England were not far removed from this pattern. The American universities, the modern British universities and, since the 1930s, the Australian universities, have had a stratum of full-time administrators. Some of them had been university teachers but they ceased to be so on becoming full-time administrators, appointed for long terms, and others were never university teachers.

The amount of paper-work has grown as universities have become more dependent on and accountable in greater detail to governments for the support which they receive and as every new research project requires a new application of many pages and in many copies. More administrators are needed to deal with these papers and to certify them before passing them on to the next higher level of authority. Governments demand more information about what is being done to observe their regulations, and not only regarding the expenditure of funds which they have awarded to universities. The more exacting the laws regulating the conditions of employment of industrial and commercial employees, the more records the universities have to keep and the greater the number of non-academic staff they require for the purpose because the universities are employers of manual, custodial and clerical workers, just as are private, industrial and commercial enterprises. The care of animals used for biomedical research has increasingly aroused the concern of governments and hence more records must be kept; the universities must employ persons who will watch over and enforce conformity with laws and decrees of government concerning the care of experimental animals.

It is in the nature of bureaucracies to extend themselves. More tasks, quite reasonable tasks are discovered; it then becomes necessary to increase the administrative staff for that purpose. So, at least, it seems to administrators. As a result, the administrative staffs proliferate and academics find themselves surrounded on all sides by administrators, who want forms filled out, who wish to have their permission sought to do things for which older academics do not recall having had to seek permission. Rules, forms and "channels" become more prominent; informal understandings and conventions become less prominent in the administration of universities.

In some universities, the activities of teachers are subjected to minute scrutiny in order to assure maximal "productivity". The amount of time spent in class-rooms and in consultation with students is expressed in "contact-hours" and a certain number of "contact-hours" is stipulated as obligatory. There have even been indications on the part of governmental officials that teachers should be present in the university during "working hours", contrary to the traditional view that teachers should be free, apart from scheduled classes and "office hours", to spend their time wherever they found it most convenient to do their academic work.

With all this proliferation of administration and of administrators around research and teaching, these two central activities are, at their hearts, untouched. In liberal-democratic countries with academic freedom and university autonomy, once a scientist or scholar is in his class-room or seminar room or laboratory or library study, he is, as he has been for a long time, the master of his own intellectual actions. Nevertheless, he does not always feel that way; instead he feels himself hemmed in, pushed and pulled hither and thither, by administrators who are alien in spirit to his vital intellectual concerns. This fosters a sense of alienation from "the university" which he sees as dominated by the bureaucracy and in essential antagonism to what he thinks are his main obligations.

The Financially Straitened University: The growth of the "mass university" in the period after the Second World War would not have been possible without munificent financial support by governments. Scientific research has, for the most part, been supported by governmental bodies separate from those which supply the funds for capital and current costs of conducting the instructional activities of universities. Many new universities were founded and were equipped at great expense; large teaching staffs were appointed. In a number of countries, and most of all in the United States, funds provided by public bodies were supplemented by funds provided by private bodies and individuals. It became possible through these greatly increased funds to appoint more teachers, to construct new buildings, to purchase more and more powerful and refined scientific equipment, to purchase more books for libraries, to appoint more administrators and to increase the services and amenities for students, as well as to pay the fees for many of them and even to pay for their maintenance. Grants for tuition fees and maintenance were supplemented in the United States by loans from the federal government.

The easy and unprecedented availability of funds from governments and philanthropic foundations caused a euphoric attitude to grow among university teachers and administrators. Young persons shared this euphoria to some extent. All were confident of the future. Unceasing public favour and largesse were taken as assured. The universities went on increasing the size of their academic and administrative staffs and adding to their physical plant with relatively little anxiety that the resources to pay the salaries, support the research and maintain the buildings and equipment might cease to grow or even diminish. Nevertheless that is what has happened. The universities in most countries have had in the past decade to reckon with the cessation of the growth in their income, and many higher educational institutions in the United States and an increasing number in Europe have seen their budgets decrease. Demographic changes have contributed to this but more important has been the governmental decision to reduce the allocation of funds for education at all levels.

We need not concern ourselves with why nearly all governments in liberal-democratic societies have tapered off their enthusiasm for universities. They have certainly not ceased to expect the universities to meet all the demands for training, service and research which had been directed at them previously.

Governmental allocation of funds for scientific research, although ceasing to grow at the same rate as in the several decades which followed the Second World War, have continued to grow slightly or to remain approximately constant. The funds for instruction, the "regular" budget from which salaries of teachers are paid, have stopped increasing and in some cases declined. This has meant a marked reduction in the numbers of new appointments and this in turn has meant that young scientists and scholars who have recently completed their studies have found it very difficult to obtain appointments.

As part of the rapid expansion of the 1950s and 1960s, many persons were appointed to permanent tenure at early ages or were granted such tenure fairly shortly. In consequence of this, universities for the coming years are amply and expensively provided with teachers in most subjects at the higher levels of salary and with a large number of retirements scheduled to fall due only towards the end of the present decade or later. Until then, there will be serious obstacles to the careers of young aspirants to academic careers. This has also aggravated the situation since mistakes in appointment committed in the period of great expansion cannot be corrected by new appointments of more able young persons. The damage done by earlier misjudgements cannot under these conditions be undone. Any postponement of the age of retirement such as has recently been enacted into law in the United States will reinforce these obstacles.

This has very discouraging effects, not only on those who have acquired the qualifications for an academic career and have in some cases already begun those careers, but also on those who would otherwise be inclined to seek those qualifications. There is, in short, the danger of a loss of an academic generation. This is a personal tragedy for the individuals so affected and an obstacle to the growth of knowledge which is dependent on the creative powers of younger workers in each field. It is injurious to the universities in many other ways. It widens the always threatening cleavage between senior and junior teachers. The threat of redundancy generates anxiety about personal fates and about whole courses of study, especially in fields in which there are few students and which are relatively costly to maintain. All this distracts young academics from the tasks of teaching and research and it worries older academics who are solicitous about their subjects, their institutions and their professions.

In the countries under discussion here, governments played a decisive role in the promotion of the expansion of the numbers of students and academic staffs and in the establishment of new universities. The academics welcomed the expansion with much enthusiasm. They were very exhilarated by the increase in the size of the teaching staffs of their departments and they gave little thought to the duration of expansion and the possibility and consequences of its cessation. Incumbent professors, particularly the older generation, should have thought of the morrow. It should have been readily apparent to them that the expansion could not continue indefinitely.

The University in the Eye of Publicity: For much of their history, universities were not widely noticed in their societies. The mass of the population ignored them, except for the small groups of employees who served them in various menial capacities, local shopkeepers, innkeepers and lodging-house keepers who gained a livelihood from the students, and the townspeople who were occasionally made aware of them by rampaging undergraduates in altercations between town and gown. Some students engaged in revolutionary and nationalistic political activities in France and Germany but they were more attended to by the police than by the wider public. The major activities of universities were not of much interest to the working or the middle classes. The fame of universities existed mainly for academics and for learned persons outside the universities and for the rulers of society:

the universities were very remote from and shadowy to the workaday larger world.

This state of affairs had persisted over many centuries. Even after the development of the popular press in the second half of the nineteenth century, the universities received no treatment in its columns. The superior press published brief articles and letters by professors, announced jubilees and deaths. Some professors entered on political careers but this did not attract attention to the universities. It is really only in the twentieth century that universities became "news". The ceremonial dedication of major academic buildings and scientific installations and spectacular achievements touching local pride also received some attention. In English-speaking countries, athletic competitions and games began to attract popular attention. In the present century, scientific discoveries, archaeological excavations, great steps in surgery and medical therapy began to be reported outside the scientific press. But even though such subjects began to be treated in the press, there seems to have been no "science writers" in popular newspapers before the First World War.

The universities did not seek publicity. It did not occur to academics and university administrators to seek it. Individual academics did not yearn to be "in the news". American universities in the 1920s did employ "press officers" but their task was to prevent the universities from being placed before the public eye when some possibly embarrassing event occurred; it is unlikely that any Continental European university had a press officer. There was no call for such a person. The press, apart from the handful of superior newspapers, did not concern itself with universities and was not interested in receiving "press releases" from "public relations officers" of universities. The wider public, even in the middle classes, had no interest in reading about universities in the daily press; the working classes scarcely knew that universities existed and had little interest in learning what they were. Occasionally universities drew the attention of the press; the undergraduate debate on the "defence of king and country" in the Oxford Union, the conflict over the cancellation of Bertrand Russell's appointment at the City College of New York, the troubles of Professor John Anderson at Sydney or of Scott Nearing at Pennsylvania and of McKeen Cattell at Columbia were *causes célèbres* and very much out of the ordinary run of events.

A very dramatic change took place after the Second World War. Universities entered much more extensively into the consciousness of their contemporaries. The increased numbers of students, the increased appearance of university teachers as advisers, the successes of academic scientists during the war, the brushing of universities by Soviet espionage, the implication of a small number of university teachers in espionage and the rumours and accusations of the connections of larger numbers in such activities as well as the general conviction that universities held the keys to a happier, more prosperous future made newspapers begin to attend more seriously to the activities of universities. Universities became, in a sense, part of the "beat" of newspapermen. The achievements and the claims of scientists became "news". The fortunes of the universities became "newsworthy"; the activities of their students, the opinions of their presidents and the views of their teachers about all sorts of public events became material for journalists. The social sciences joined the natural sciences as "news"; the natural scientists reported their discoveries, sometimes through press conferences which they or their universities convoked. Social scientists were frequent sources of assessments of contemporary economic, social and political questions. Legislative investigations repeatedly summoned academics as expert witnesses.

University administrators were in step with this mood. Since the universities were being conducted in a more and more costly fashion, funds from governments, private foundations and individuals had to be raised—in different proportions in different countries. To attract and hold the favour of legislators and political leaders, university administrators, singly and collectively, had to try to reach them; the printed press, radio and television seemed to be the appropriate instruments for this. Thus, both sides seemed to approach each other, the universities approaching journalists in order to gain attention and appreciation for their achievements and an understanding of their problems, journalists approaching the university as a source of interesting news.

The student disturbances of the 1960s and 1970s made universities into even more eagerly observed sources of dramatic "news"; in fact, the publicity which was so readily available helped to extend the student disturbances nationally and internationally. The student disruptors' desire for publicity was in fact one manifestation of the quest for publicity which has become very widespread in Western societies.

Many academics seek publicity for themselves and their work. In some universities, teachers who are in dispute with their colleagues, break the confidentiality of the proceedings of governing and appointive bodies by "leaking" to the press. The press is drawn into academic disagreements and aggravates them. Aggrieved members of the universities turn to the press as well as to the courts to vindicate their cause and to remedy the wrongs which they think they have suffered.

Confidentiality, which had long been regarded as right in university proceedings, is no longer thought to be so, especially in the United States. Courts in two separate American jurisdictions have ordered members of appointive bodies to disclose how they voted for a particular candidate. The federal government has legislated a prohibition of confidentiality in the assessment of students and the federal bureaucracy demands that confidential assessments of candidates for appointments be taken into their custody. (Once in the possession of the federal government, these assessments are open to anyone who wishes to obtain copies of them under the Freedom of Information Act.)

Some of the publicity given to significant scientific and scholarly discoveries is desirable as a form of public education and it might also be beneficial to the universities by enabling ordinary citizens to learn about and to appreciate their achievements. But much of it is a distraction to many of the academics who seek it, some of whom come to regard a broad publicity as a good in itself; others do so because it enables them to raise their prestige in the academic world. Some of them regard it, rather than the judgement of their qualified colleagues, as evidence of the merit of their achievements.

The "Research University": The idea of the modern university was shaped by Wilhelm von Humboldt who thought that the university should be a place of scientific and scholarly research where young persons were inducted into and educated through research. The "unity of teaching and research" formulated this idea, which reached into the life of universities throughout the world. It guided the reform of existing universities and it set the pattern of newly established ones. Although some universities placed greater emphasis on research and others placed more emphasis on teaching, it was not generally believed that these two activities were in a mutually exclusive relationship with each other.

The situation changed after the Second World War. Research in the United States became in some of the leading universities more prized than teaching, particularly the teaching of undergraduates. Research came to be regarded as the primary obligation; the desire to do research spread to higher educational institutions which had previously placed primary emphasis on teaching. It was not difficult to understand why this change took place after the great triumphs of scientific research during the Second World War. The availability of large sums for the support of research, the high public prestige of research and the tendency to base decisions on academic appointments and promotions on achievements and promise in research all placed research at the top of the agenda of the university teacher. Many persons who would have preferred teaching to research felt they had to do research. Many were swept into research by the strong currents of academic opinion.

Under conditions such as these, which were very favourable for research, universities which were already distinguished in research shot further ahead of the others in their accomplishments. They were the most esteemed and the most talked about. Other universities seeking to hold their own in the increasingly acute competition for eminence also placed the criteria of achievement in research in the forefront. Those who did not succeed in research were regarded by others and themselves as inferior. Many individuals who did not have a very strong propensity to do research felt themselves compelled to do it. Whatever the scientific or scholarly significance of their results, the activity of research itself became a condition of minimal academic self-respect.

The disturbances in the universities caused by the agitation of the 1960s and early 1970s aroused some uncertainties about this elevation of research in the hierarchy of academic values. They led some academics to turn against the academic ethos and to denounce the obligation to do research, to deny the possibility of objectivity in research and to deride the devotion to science and scholarship as no more than an "ideology". Others reacting in the opposite direction were led to feel aversion from universities, to reduce their teaching and to concentrate on research and to working with graduate students.

Although European universities did not fall prey to the classification which separated "research universities" from "other universities", the conditions of the "mass university", the student agitation and the subsequent university reforms alienated many teachers from the existing pattern which coupled research and teaching. In Germany, the "Humboldt-pattern" was declared to be no longer practicable; research, it has been said, can no longer be done by teachers in the ordinary universities. According to this idea ordinary universities should concentrate on teaching; special universities should be provided for the conduct of research.

From the high value accorded to research, it follows that the university teacher tends to be assessed in accordance with his achievements in research. Achievements in research are easier to assess than are achievements in teaching; the results of research are visible in published works, the results of teaching cannot be seen adequately either in marks on examinations or in the approval of students for the pedagogical merit of a particular teacher. For these reasons all teachers and especially younger teachers, wishing to assure their reappointment and promotion to permanence of tenure, often engage in research with an intensity which goes much beyond their intellectual interest in the problems they study. Even where the university teacher is deeply interested in the problem of his research, he often feels himself additionally compelled in his research by the belief that his success in its completion, publication and acceptance will affect his academic career, either in the university in which he holds an appointment or in one to which he wishes to be invited. This state has two consequences which are worth noting; one is that it calls forth additional effort in the talented inducing them to devote themselves to research with a degree of concentration which they might not otherwise demand of themselves. In such cases, the demanding atmosphere and considerations of advancement in the academic career add a beneficial impetus to the production of work of high quality. The other consequence is not so beneficial. This occurs when the individual who might be an excellent teacher and who might take seriously the necessity of "keeping up" with publications in his subject but who has little desire to do research is constrained in order to secure his reappointment or advancement to do research in which he has less interest and aptitude than he has in teaching. Inasmuch as most universities nowadays wish to be "research universities" and hence regard achievements in research as paramount criteria in appointments and promotion, many persons the results of whose research add little that is valuable to the stock of knowledge are forced, willy-nilly, to be "published" scholars and scientists.

The widespread desire of administrators and senior academics that their universities be research universities, is reinforced by the prevailing methods of granting financial support for research by bodies external to the universities. In the United States, at least, the universities have become dependent on grants for particular research projects in order to obtain the funds needed to pay the salaries of many of the members of their academic staffs. Teachers are pressed therefore to seek grants for research in order to help to pay their salaries. This increases the pressure on individuals to engage more intensively in research than they otherwise might do.

The elevation of the criterion of the publication of the results of research to a dominant position creates special difficulties for younger academics. Although the publication of short papers in scientific and scholarly journals is relatively easy because of the large number of journals in every field, the publication of books and monographs is less so. The increased costs of printing, paper and binding have greatly raised the costs of publication of academic books and thereby reduced their sale. Publishers are therefore reluctant to invest their resources in the production of books which will have an excessively small market. Thus, while universities concerned to enhance their reputation as "research universities" attribute more and more importance to the publication of books and monographs as well as shorter papers, the obstacles to the publication of such larger works by younger scholars have grown in recent years. To be sure, many books and monographs still continue to be published both by commercial publishing firms and by university presses.

Another of the consequences of the increased emphasis on research is that teachers have become more interested in and more attentive to what goes on in the "profession", constituted by those who are doing research in their discipline regardless of where they are, than they are in their colleagues within their own university or in the problems of their own university. It is inherent in the present-day organisation of learning that teachers inform themselves about what is being accomplished in their own field of study, wherever that work is being done. A teacher who does not keep up with current work in his field is giving his students less than they should have from him. But, granting this inevitable and desirable external direction of intellectual interest, the great weight laid on achievement in research as evidence of success in the academic career has been associated with an increased indifference to the affairs of one's own university. It is obviously possible to maintain a dual loyalty and many university teachers are able to do so. Nevertheless, the balance of concern has shifted outward to the detriment of academic citizenship.

The Disaggregated University: A university has to have some minimal institutional arrangements for decisions regarding the allocation of resources among its parts, for the performance of certain services common to the whole university such as the maintenance of buildings, grounds and libraries, for the purchase of equipment and supplies, for the keeping of records, and for the acquisition, administration and expenditure of financial resources. All these activities are services to the individual members of teaching staffs, to the departments and the student body. These arrangements do not, as such, require a sense of membership in a corporate entity on the part of the beneficiaries of these various services; they do not inevitably require or give rise to a sense of solidarity on the part of the teachers with each other, and of their students with each other and with their teachers. They do not necessarily entail a sense of responsibility on the part of each member towards the other members of the university nor do they necessarily generate stimulating intellectual interaction among the individual members of the teaching staff, or the intellectual influence of some individuals on other individuals within the teaching staff. The administrative functions of a university do not involve the dependence of each individual on the silent but significant proximity of so many other persons engaged in the same undertaking of discovering and teaching reliable knowledge. All of these intellectual functions depend on but do not necessarily arise from the bare existence of the university as a legal entity and as an administrative machine performing indispensable services for its members. Nevertheless, a well-functioning university is more than a legally recognised corporation and an administrative machine; it is an intellectual corporation.

Probably no university has ever been completely without conflict or egotism; no university has ever been the object of the solicitude of all its members, each recognising the intellectual benefits which he receives from his membership in it. Universities have always been divided into faculties, departments, colleges and other segments. Universities have always been cut across by the lines of generation and ranks. There have always been rivalries among teachers and cleavages between teachers and students. All this notwithstanding, universities which have a single campus and where teachers live near their universities and have studies in them are likely to have more corporate spirit than universities in which faculties are scattered spatially and where teachers live far from the university, appearing there only to teach and absenting themselves at all other times. The universities of Latin Europe have been the most dispersed in this respect. But even where there was wide spatial dispersion, it was not decisive, and the formation of an intellectual corporate spirit did occur to some extent. Outstanding universities have always approximated wholes which have been greater than the sums of their parts.

In the past few decades, the internal unity of universities has been under strain. When the student bodies of universities expanded in size and more funds were available for the appointment of teachers and for research, not only were new recruits to the academic profession brought in, but academics who had already entered upon their careers moved about from university to university in search of more stimulating, more pleasing, more remunerative and more honorific appointments. The expansion of the number of universities increased the intensity of the game of "musical chairs". Teachers shifted from university to university to a far greater degree than they had when universities were increasing very little in either number or size. It is no criticism of the right of individuals to seek appointments which are more suitable to their talents, tastes and interests and which are more remunerative and honorific, to observe that the movements sometimes have an unsettling effect on the universities those individuals leave or join. In general, a restless seeking for opportunities to go elsewhere has a weakening effect on the morale of a university; it is also a consequence of a weakness of morale or attachment to and care for the institution where the individual in question holds an appointment.

Specialisation has similar effects. The unceasing advancement of specialisation in scientific and scholarly research, coupled with the greater attention given to research have caused individual scientists and scholars to be more interested in what colleagues in their own fields of specialisation outside their own universities are doing than they are in what is being done by their colleagues in their own universities who are working in neighbouring or remoter fields of scientific or scholarly enquiry. Furthermore, the greatly increased size of departments has reduced the likelihood of talking to persons "outside" one's own department within the same university. The newer modes of providing support for research projects by extra-university patrons has also a tendency to cause academics to have their minds focused more intently on the world outside their own universities.

The centrifugal inclinations of individual academics in universities in the provinces are nourished especially in countries in which life in the capital city is very much more attractive than life in the provinces. In such countries as France and Italy, there are many professors who hold appointments in the provinces but who live in the capital, appearing at their universities only at the hours when they are scheduled to teach.

The tradition which provides that only deans and heads of institutes have rooms at the university in which to work and to receive students and colleagues, also serves to disconnect the teachers from each other, from their students and from the university as an intellectual corporation. These factors have certainly not been insuperable, as many Continental universities have shown, but they have hampered the unity of the university.

The existence of a large proportion of students who have no interest either in their academic studies or in the collective life of their university has also the effect of diminishing the inward direction of affections and attachments. The mass university has brought into the university many young persons whose foremost and perhaps exclusive aim is to obtain a degree and to enter a remunerative occupation. These students have little intellectual interest and they are often not open to sentiments of attachment to their particular university.

The new university laws in Continental Europe have also added to the centrifugal tendencies within universities. These laws have declared—more explicitly in some countries than in others—that the different sections of the university have "interests" which are in principle incompatible with each other. The students are said to have interests which are antithetical to the interests of teachers, the interests of young teachers in the lower ranks are treated as antithetical to the interests of older teachers in the higher ranks. Administrative and custodial employees are also said to have their own distinctive interests, which are said to be different from the interests of teachers of different ranks and of students. That is why, according to this legislation, each of these interests must have its own spokesmen. According to this conception of the university, justice is to be done to these various divergent interests by giving them representation in governing bodies, the primary task of which is to arrive at compromises among these fundamentally conflicting interests. This enactment in legislation of the idea that the university is a constellation of conflicting interests has deepened and made more rigid the conflicts which upset the university during the time of the student disturbances; it has not reconciled them. The legislation based on this idea has added one more seriously disaggregative impulsion to the already existing tendencies towards disaggregation arising from large numbers, specialisation, external financial support for particular research projects, and the intensification of attention to government and politics which is characteristic of all modern societies.

As the central governments in all modern societies have acquired more and more tasks and powers, their constituent institutions have all become much less self-contained. One of the many consequences is that these institutions dwell within themselves much less than they used to and are more turned outwards into the arena of political controversy and governmental action than was the case prior to the Second World War. University teachers and students have become politicised, which means being more inclined to give precedence in attention to things external to the university and to bring those external matters into the university. Since politics is by its nature contentious and partisan, the strengthening of such attitudes in universities has disaggregative results.

The University with Shaken Morale: Whole universities, particular departments and individuals have from time to time suffered crises of confidence. The loss of a number of eminent members, severe internal conflicts, distracting misfortunes and sometimes the stagnant state of a discipline, have all at one time or another injuriously affected the pride and self-confidence of the individual or the institution. There are disciplines in which the practitioners think that the discipline has not fulfilled its promise, or cannot go forward to new tasks and new problems and techniques. Withdrawal, resentful criticism of their disciplines and an arbitrary thrashing about are characteristic of such an intellectual condition. Disciplines of which their practitioners were once proud and confident can fall within a few years into this state.

In recent years this has been somewhat more common in the social sciences and the humanities than in the natural and technological sciences. The change has occurred mostly in the younger and middle generations. Some of them have felt that they made a mistake in entering the academic career. Some of them have thought that there is nothing of significance in their subjects. They have been led in some instances into political activity as a way of doing something significant. Some, in recent years, have come to think that their subjects as generally practised over the past several generations are just "ideologies" supporting the "ruling classes" and serving as instruments of "imperialism" and "colonialism". Others have attempted to prove that as hitherto practised, their entire discipline is a fraud. There has been much denunciation of their professional colleagues and particularly of some of the acclaimed leaders in their disciplines. They sometimes have sought the admiration of their more antinomian students by denouncing their subjects and disciplines in class.

This situation was sorely aggravated by the student disorders of the late 1960s and the early 1970s. The disaffection of the students shook the moorings of some teachers who did not have sufficient confidence to withstand the muddle-headed attacks on their subjects which some of the more vociferous students were making. They had never previously been asked to construct such a defence and it is not surprising that they did not have one at their fingertips. The traditions of their discipline had existed and interested them and that had been enough. But once they looked critically at the research which they had done, they decided that it had not been satisfactory. Some of them concluded that they had chosen the wrong career. Others concluded that universities were a "racket". This kind of demoralisation is to some extent a reaction against the overbearing pride and optimism which some university teachers felt about their subjects during the period of demographic and financial expansion.

The Persistence of the University as a Centre of Learning: The phenomena which we have called the "mass university", the "service university", the "political university", the "governmentally controlled university", the "bureaucratic university", the "research university", the university seeking the "eye of publicity" and the "disaggregated university" are undeniable features of academic life of the past third of a century. In some cases, they have been present for a longer time, in others for a considerably shorter time; they are by no means equally present in all universities within any single country; there are also differences in the extent to which they affect the university systems of the various countries with which we deal. Still, despite variations, these features in various combinations have affected the situations of university teachers quite tangibly. Each of them has placed a strain, in various ways, on the performance by university teachers of their fundamental and central tasks of teaching and research. They have in extreme cases rendered the performance of these tasks very difficult. They have all contributed to changing the situation of the university teacher from what it was in Western countries in the period of somewhat more than a century prior to the outbreak of the Second World War.

The situation of universities within the larger world of learning has also changed. A great deal of research is now being done outside the universities. Research in the laboratories of industrial firms and governmental departments has grown greatly. Independent research institutes, privately and governmentally supported and doing a certain amount of the basic and theoretical research which had been in most countries practically a monopoly of universities have become much more common. Institutes of advanced study which were extremely rare before the Second World War have become fairly numerous and have become havens into which scientists and scholars escape from the distractions of the mass university and the other aspects of university life in recent years. (At one time universities themselves provided exactly such havens for undistracted study and reflection.) The training of a small number of graduate students has been provided by a few independent, industrial and governmental research institutions; in this respect, however, the universities still enjoy an approximate monopoly.

Despite these erosions and arrogations, universities still remain the major centres of learning in their respective societies. The pursuit of fundamental knowledge still goes on within them with great intensity. Much else goes on there, too. Not all of it is by any means practically useful or intellectually valuable; some of it is pedantic and "academic" in the pejorative sense of the term. Very important research is still done in universities and the induction of students into the works of the mind, to the mastery of principles of understanding and habits of thought likewise goes on there. These vital functions without which no society can be a good society are nevertheless exposed to distraction and constrictions. They can still be performed and effectively performed as long as university teachers are aware of their obligations and are eager to carry them out, out of the conviction of the value of their tasks and out of love for the knowledge which they possess and pursue.

The carrying out of these obligations will be well served if university teachers are reminded from time to time of the commitments which they have taken upon themselves when they entered upon the academic profession. The following observations attempt to clarify these commitments and to draw out some of their implications.

THE ACADEMIC OBLIGATIONS OF UNIVERSITY TEACHERS

All the particular obligations of university teachers to students, to colleagues, to their universities and to their respective societies derive their binding force fundamentally from their obligations to ascertain what is true in their research, study and teaching, to assess scrupulously what has been handed down as true and to cultivate and propagate an active quest for truth as an ideal.

The Obligation of Knowledge: To be in a university postulates a common commitment on the part of all of its members to a belief that some grounds for the acceptance and espousal of a proposition or conception are better than other grounds.

Teaching and research are about the pursuit and transmission of truths, the methods of distinguishing between truth and error, so far as that is humanly possible, and the distinction between fallacious and valid evidence and argument. To speak of knowledge is to accept the validity of methods of acquiring and assessing evidence; it is to speak of reason and of rigour in its exercise. A teacher who knowingly presents to his students erroneous and baseless beliefs while purporting to present them as demonstrated knowledge is clearly departing from his primary obligation, regardless of whether he intends to curry the favour of established authorities or to overturn them and regardless of whether he wishes to please his audience or is simply careless.

A university teacher who knowingly or carelessly presents a false account of his observations in a report of his research is no less culpable than one who deliberately teaches false accounts of the subject for which he is responsible.

Hence we may say that the first obligation of the university teacher is to the truth about the subject-matters which he teaches or investigates. Of course, to determine what is true about an important matter can be extremely difficult. What is thought to be the truth about a particular topic or subject-matter is inevitably subject to change but the changes are not arbitrary. The changes are subject to disciplined methods; they are subject to the substantive tradition of the subject, even though that too undergoes changes with every increment to and revision of the stock of knowledge about any particular topic. There are also huge grey areas where reliable knowledge is patently not available. These are the areas where it is very tempting to a teacher to heed his predilections more than his intellectual scruples. But these situations impose the obligations of hard work, good judgement, scrupulousness and self-discipline. The apparently definitive areas of knowledge—the black, well-established areas—must be faced with a readiness to change one's belief about them because even though they look final, they are bound not to turn out to be so as knowledge grows. The grey areas, if they are important, are the areas where new research is called for and the judgement of his equally qualified peers in his own university and elsewhere throughout the world of learning is needed to keep the university teacher on his mettle. Much teaching has to be done in these grey areas, indeed many disciplines fall almost entirely within the grey areas; in teaching them to students less experienced in the subject than himself, making them aware of such uncertainties is obligatory for the teacher.

To present as an established truth what is nothing more than an unsubstantiated opinion or a tentative hypothesis is nearly as great a defection from the obligation of a university teacher as it is knowingly to put forward a false proposition as true or to disregard the existence of available new evidence which throws doubt on what has previously been accepted. The teacher, of course, will inevitably have to exercise a degree of responsible personal judgement in such matters; he is not a calculating machine. He is entitled to express his doubts about the supposed new evidence, to express his own conviction that a still tentative hypothesis will turn out to be true. Inevitably, he will sometimes be wrong on both these points. All that is demanded from him is honesty and modesty about what is and what is not at a given time, seriously controversial and about what is simply not known. This does not entail that he ought to become a Pyrrhonian sceptic. There are better grounds for holding some views than there are for holding others, even when they are subject to revision. He should help his students to learn to make such comparative judgements about competing interpretations and to learn to be ready to revise their judgements when better evidence and reasons are available.

The situation is little different when the university teacher is engaged in a role involving his knowledge outside the university. Perhaps the situation is more testing morally when the teacher is acting outside the university because the standards of truthfulness generally insisted on in political controversy or in the public discussions of alternatives of policy are less exigent. In the heat of controversy, the temptations of triumph are very powerful but the obligations to discriminate between what one has good grounds for taking to be true and what is doubtful are not less great than they are in academic settings.

The obligation of a university teacher to discover and enunciate the truth about the particular objects of his investigation entails a corresponding obligation to investigate whatever he regards as important intellectually and practically. This means that he has an obligation, while respecting the methods or rules of enquiry, to refuse to accept the domination of current popular, political and academic prejudices regarding what it is permissible to investigate. The fact that a subject is "unpopular" must not be allowed to deter a scrupulous scientist or scholar from studying it, as long as he adheres to the methods of scientific or scholarly investigation. It does not mean that an academic may disregard the obligations which govern, for example, experimentation on human beings or which forbid damage to the persons studied or to those who are working with him, nor is he exempt from the obligations regarding publication such as submission to review of his results by his professional peers. It does mean that he must insist on his right to the freedom to investigate whatever he deems to be important.

The obligation to promote the growth of knowledge implies an obligation to share with colleagues the knowledge produced through research. A scientist or scholar is not under obligation to disclose his results to his colleagues before he has satisfied himself that they are as sound as he can make them but once he has satisfied himself in that regard, he is under obligation to publish them in such a way that colleagues can study and assess them. The obligation to knowledge is met through investigation and "open" publication; secrecy is alien to the obligation of university teachers. There might be exceptional situations in which certain particular results obtained by a scientist working on a project supported by government might be kept secret after consultation between the scientist who has made the discovery in question and a qualified government official but it must be treated as an exception. The general obligation is to undertake research which is publishable. The scientist who does research which he knows in advance must be kept secret should do such research in a governmental laboratory and not in a university.

His obligation to knowledge does not require that the university teacher become an author of large numbers of scientific or scholarly papers and enough books to fill a small shelf. Universities are institutions of research and teaching but this does not imply that every teacher must be so active in research that practically all his time when he is not in a class-room should be spent doing "original" research in a laboratory or a library, or "in the field" if that is the kind of research done in his discipline. Nor should a teacher regard it as an obligation to exceed his colleagues in the number of his published works.

To do research does inevitably entail the multiplication of works which repeat one another in some respects. New research, even very original research, must inevitably have its point of departure in previously done research. Works by the same author repeat each other and so do works by different authors. Originality is scarcer than the number of publications. Yet the situation is hard to overcome. Research should be published if it meets the standards of responsible referees. Under present arrangements of financial support, every project which is supported has to culminate in publication. If it does not, then the research worker in question will be unable to obtain financial support for his research in the future and he will be discredited. The urge to publish in order to contribute to the growth of knowledge, to gain respect for one's achievements and to advance in one's career is reinforced by the expectations of the patrons of research. Research, the results of which are not communicated to others, cannot in the nature of the case be a contribution to knowledge.

The urge to publish has grown with the increased prestige of research in the academic world and with the attention given to lists of publications as a criterion in appointments, including reappointments and promotions. The quantity of published works is easier to estimate than the quality of those works and teachers who compose with some fluency sometimes become indiscriminate in what they publish. Nevertheless, research workers must attempt to publish the results of their investigations if they are up to standard. Publications of scientific and scholarly works must be accompanied by truthful attribution of their authorship. Since careers in the academic profession are oriented towards the recognition and reward of individual achievement, plagiary of the work of others and claiming credit for the work of others infringe on the derivative obligation to acknowledge the achievements of colleagues. The presentation of reports of observations made by others regardless of whether they have been published, as if they were observations made by oneself is a defection of this derivative obligation. Claiming the exclusive authorship of a work done in collaboration or claiming primary authorship of a work to which one's contribution was marginal is a grave impropriety.

The service of knowledge entails not only the discovery of new knowledge but also the transmission of the best of established knowledge to students. No teacher should allow himself to go on teaching as if the body of knowledge in his field has remained constant. Even in humanistic fields where there is an approximate canon of works to be taught and studied, new commentaries and interpretations require both the recurrent re-study of the canonical works and a well-informed awareness of the best interpretations of the works. Of course, to be abreast of "the literature" should not be confused with fashionableness. The growth of the body of knowledge in any particular field is not furthered by the espousal of fashionable topics and interpretations. Neither the body of knowledge in the field nor the students who study it are benefited by the multiplication of trivial or fashionable publications. The serious teacher will, of course, attempt to inform himself adequately about recent publications in his field of scholarship but as much to give his students the best that is known as well as to protect them intellectually from nonsense which they might otherwise accept.

Research is obligatory for those who can do it; it should not be regarded as equally obligatory for those who show little talent for it. For such persons the obligation regarding research is to attend to its results and to incorporate them into teaching to help their students to understand what research in their field is and to assimilate them into the outlook which pervades research. Those academics who do little or no research are under obligation to pay close attention in their teaching to the results of research in their field.

Obligations to Students: The Humboldtian ideal of the unity of teaching and research remains a valid one. The university is not a research institute. It is an institution of teaching and research. Teaching is as important as research in a university. In principle, all persons holding regular academic appointments in a university should do both teaching and research but not necessarily always in the same proportions. Teachers in liberal arts colleges may legitimately distribute their time differently between teaching and research than teachers in universities where there is a greater emphasis on research. Some teachers might concentrate on the teaching of the most advanced students, the supervision of graduate students and the conduct of research-seminars. There may even be a small number of "research-professorships" but their multiplication is contrary to the requirements of the academic ethic. A university in which teachers shirk their pedagogical obligation in order to advance "their own work", as if their sole obligation is to do research, infringes on the academic ethic. Properly understood, "their own work" includes teaching.

The ideal of the formation of the mind—and character—by research must also apply to teaching. Teaching is not merely the transmission of a body of substantive, factual or theoretical knowledge. It must aim at conveying understanding of the fundamental truths in the subject and the methods of enquiry and testing characteristic of their subject.

It should go without saying that negligence in the performance of pedagogical tasks ought to be abhorrent to a university teacher. It is not only a puritanical praise of assiduity or the ordinary principle of commercial honesty which asserts that the acceptance of payment entails the delivery of the goods paid for that requires industrious preparation of teaching. A teacher cannot hope to arouse the spirit of enquiry in his students or to get them to see the need for care and imagination if his teaching is desultory. This implies, among other things, that the teacher must inform himself of the best scientific and scholarly achievement of the best workers in the subject which he is teaching. To do less is to present to the students as unchallenged truths what might have been subjected to severe criticism. Given the present volume of production of scientific and scholarly works, this ideal can probably not be completely achieved. This does not make the striving for it less obligatory.

The postulate that the university is an institution, the primary obligation of which is the discovery and teaching of important and serious scientific and scholarly truths does not require that teachers should eschew the assertion of their political and ethical beliefs before their pupils. It does however mean that university teachers must avoid allowing it to appear that their political or ethical statements are scientific or scholarly statements; it also means that they must not allow what they put forward as truthful knowledge to be determined by their political or ethical ideals and sympathies. University teachers must also avoid discriminating among their students on the basis of the students' own political or ethical ideals and sympathies. (It goes without saying that for teachers to discriminate in the assessment of their students on the basis of the students' sex, religion, pigmentation, ethnic or social-class origin is absolutely antithetical to the academic ethic.)

The only immediate guarantee of the university teacher's observance of his obligation to teach what is true and important to his students is the seriousness with which he takes his calling, his belief in the value of the knowledge that he teaches and his conviction that the truth about his subject-matter is eminently worth knowing and propagating. Conformity with this obligation can come only from strictness of conscience and conviction of the worthwhileness of the intellectual activity in which he is engaged. The teacher's conviction is manifested in his patent seriousness and pleasure in the intellectual value of his own subject; his commitment to knowledge is evident in his tone. It is this perception of these dispositions as much as the substantive knowledge which the teaching imparts that arouses and compels students.

The teacher has to be careful not to fall into dogmatism in the exposition of his subject or to attempt improperly to exercise influence on his students by demanding that they become adherents of his own particular substantive and methodological point of view. He must enable his students to know that his own point of view is not the only reasonable one and that other scientists or scholars have different interpretations and approaches, of which the students should be aware. To yield to the temptation of dogmatism is to be unfaithful to the obligation to communicate the truth.

With rare exceptions, the teacher knows more about the subject he is teaching than do his students. In this respect, he has the upper hand over his students. Their only defences against intellectual exploitation are indifference and challenging questions. In most situations, especially in the earlier years of study at universities, they do not have enough knowledge to correct him and he has therefore the opportunity to take advantage of them intellectually and hence to be unfaithful to his obligations with impunity. The students might indeed render judgements on the teacher informally or in response to questionnaires but they are in fact not often in a position to assess the truthfulness or intellectual importance of what he tells them. This is especially the case if the body of readings he recommends is so chosen as to suggest that his views are universally accepted. The acceptance of the obligations which a teacher incurs from his greater possession of knowledge extends to an obligation to take seriously his students' intellectual queries and quandaries. A teacher has an obligation to be open to the students' questions about the validity of the propositions he puts forth.

The intellectual probity of a university teacher in his classroom can be reinforced by the interest of his pupils. The egg and the chicken who lays it and who is born from it are equally important to each other; so are teacher and students as far as adherence to demanding intellectual standards is concerned. The intellectual exigency of the student strengthens the seriousness of the teacher. This is the only worthwhile sense in which teachers and pupils form a mutually sustaining intellectual community. It is not an obligation of a teacher to please his students; the attempt to please the students often gives rise to supine and degrading flattery without intellectual substance. Meeting the demands of intellectually exacting students is a different and far better thing than pleasing them. The high expectations of the best prepared and most exigent students are a spur to a teacher to exert himself to meet them. Teaching which is addressed to the capacities of the lowest quartile of the student body will render the other students apathetic; apathetic students, in their turn, engender apathetic teaching. Indifferent students do not call out the best qualities of their teachers. Yet, teaching "over the heads" of the majority of the students in a class and addressing only the very best can also have a dispiriting effect. Nevertheless, teachers should try to make their students extend themselves intellectually.

In some of the very large mass universities there has developed a widespread belief among some teachers that most of their pupils have little capacity to master the more difficult aspects of the subject taught and cannot be aroused to try to do so. The students are not taken seriously enough by these teachers; they are too often treated as children or as dullards. One of the obligations of the teacher to the students is to treat them respectfully and seriously, as if they are capable and desirous of learning difficult things. The students must be pressed to attain the highest level of knowledge which their immaturity, their capacities and their previous acquisitions permit. This is one of the obligations of the academic profession which is neglected by some teachers in many mass universities. With the emergence of higher education for much larger proportions of the generation between 18 and 22 years of age, many teachers in American and European universities, whatever their political views, have slipped into the belief that little is to be expected of their students. The result is an intellectual poverty of the syllabuses and, resulting therefrom, the intellectual poverty of the students educated according to these syllabuses.

The devotion of a university teacher to his teaching obligations is buttressed by the seriousness with which his colleagues approach their own teaching. This is why the maxim about Mark Hopkins and a student on a log is too simple. One teacher, on his own, is seldom enough. The teacher's seriousness is supported by the proximity of other serious teachers, just as the seriousness of the student is nourished by the presence of other serious students. The seriousness of his colleagues about their teaching supports him in his acceptance of an exigent standard regarding the teaching of undergraduates. The maintenance of intellectual integrity is not only a matter of strength of character but it is also a function of the immediate environment of a teacher within his department and his university. Consciences reinforce each other in intellectual matters as well as in others. The academic community thus supports the academic ethic in teaching, but it does not do so through the watchfulness expressed in the assessment of particular published works, such as occurs in the scientific community, or by polls conducted among students or by occasional visits of colleagues to classes.

It is admittedly very difficult for a teacher or his colleagues to know how well he is teaching. Some teachers have a short-term effectiveness; others exert a more permanent influence over the minds of their students. Some fill their students with well-ordered information; others arouse their curiosity. Some teachers help their students to acquire methods of observing and thinking. Formal tests of effective teaching such as conceived by education-ists, are bound to be unsatisfactory because the modes of effectiveness are numerous and some of them cannot be assessed except over a long time. An assessment of poor teaching is difficult to demonstrate except in cases of very patent defections from duty such as frequent absences from class. Obvious failure to prepare, and indifferent answers to the questions raised by students are not easy for assessors who have not observed the teacher's activity in class in a systematic manner.

One indirect way of assuring a high sense of obligation of teachers to their students is through watchfulness over the process of appointment, so as to exclude candidates who seem to be likely to be negligent about their teaching. Here, too, similar difficulties in the assessment of teaching reappear.

How then can the teacher's attitude of seriousness towards his subject-matter and towards teaching and his freedom from dogmatism be guaran-teed? There is no directly operating institutional mechanism for the observation of teaching through which the diligence, alertness, conscience and conviction of the teacher can be perceived and assessed in the way in which published scientific and scholarly works can be assessed by the judgement of peers. Persons who are outside the class-room cannot see or pass judgement on the teacher's fulfilment of his obligations to his students. Only continuous presence and adequate knowledge permit that and the students, who are the only ones continuously present, do not have adequate knowledge.

The matter comes down therefore to each teacher's own sense of obligation and his voluntary submission to it. The bearing of a conscientious teacher affects the attitude of his colleagues towards their own teaching. The sense of obligation of a teacher is strengthened by the awareness of the strength of that sense of obligation in his colleagues. This is not a tautology; it is a self-closing circle of reciprocal influences.

Students must not only be taught. They must also be assessed and they must be assessed fairly by their examiners. The assessment is important because it affects the students' chances in their subsequent studies and in admission to their professional careers. Assessment also affects the students' attitude towards their studies and towards themselves. Just assessment is as necessary for society as it is for the individual student.

Unfairness or arbitrariness in assessment of a student's performance may be a result of carelessness on the part of the examiner. It might also be a product of the examiner's personal attitude towards particular students—in those situations in which the examiner can identify the students being examined. Unfairness or arbitrariness in the assessment of the work of students might not be a result of carelessness or of the personal relationships between particular students and their teachers. Political sympathies can also have a similarly distorting effect on assessment, resulting in giving some students higher marks than their achievement merits and others lower marks.

No less important is carelessness on the part of the examiner in the maintenance of a stable standard of assessment. This is a difficult matter to control. "Double assessment" is one way of avoiding unfairness to students; this is more feasible when there is a common examination taken by the students of different teachers. The American system of either "continuous assessment" or "course examination" involves, in practically all cases, a single teacher and a single examiner who are the same person. The maintenance of a single standard under these conditions is not so easily controllable by institutional arrangements.

In the assessment of the achievement of students in mass universities which, at least in the United States, also have "continuous assessment" and "course examinations", the assessment is frequently done by "teaching assistants". Many of these assistants teach small sections of a common course. Under the latter conditions "double assessment" is possible. But where assessment deals with performance in class as well as in terminal examinations, "double assessment" is impossible.

There is no institutional arrangement for reliability guaranteeing adequacy in examining. The collective review of questions to assure that they correspond to the syllabus cannot apply where there is continuous assessment and where the syllabus of each course is determined by the person who teaches it. Numerous devices for assuring the fairness of questions can be imagined but they tend to be so cumbersome that their application would place an intolerable burden on teachers. Hence, as in the performance of obligations in teaching, the adherence to a standard which reduces to a minimum arbitrariness, dogmatism, favouritism, and excessive severity or indulgence in setting and marking examinations depends on the self-discipline and scrupulousness of the teacher-examiner.

In some universities, ecology and tradition both favour the meeting of teachers and their students outside class-rooms or laboratories. This is common in universities in which students reside on or close to the campus and where the teachers spend much of their time at the university. Even in universities in which these conditions do not obtain, opportunities for teachers to become better acquainted with their students occur at more advanced levels when classes are smaller and the intellectual interests of students and teachers are closer to each other. These relationships are often very valuable pedagogically. They afford opportunities for informal discussions about subjects beyond the limits of the syllabus. The friendly atmosphere of meetings between teachers and students is appreciated by some students; it often makes them more responsive to teaching in the class-room. The student feels more at ease in the university when he is in friendly relations with some of his teachers; the subject-matter becomes more inviting.

Informal relations of teachers with students are therefore to be welcomed. They do, however, bring with them certain dangers. One of these dangers is that in such relationships, the teacher might be inclined to favour some students over others, to give them more opportunities to enter into discussions in classes or seminars, to devote more attention to their "term-papers" or their research and also to be unfair in the assessment of the achievements of students in the sense of favouring those with whom he is friendly outside of classes over those with whom he has no such relationship. Even if the teacher does not discriminate in favour of those students whom he knows and especially those with whom he is friendly, some students will assert this; disaffection is stirred by such rumours and the students who think themselves disfavoured avoid teachers from whom they could learn. It is therefore very important that teachers attempt to avoid not only the reality but also the appearance of discrimination in favour of some students and against other students.

This is a very complicated matter and a very subtle one. It is desirable that teachers should be friendly with students and it is also inevitable that they will be more friendly with some than with others. There is nothing wrong with this in itself. It is only its intrusion into the assessment of the achievements of students in the acquisition of knowledge or its intrusion into the teaching itself that must be guarded against.

It is important too that teachers should not take advantage of their status and their power over their students. The occurrences of sexual relationships between teachers and students is certainly to be avoided. The fact that the development of sexual relations between teachers and students can result in discriminatory assessment of the student's academic achievement is only one important ground for the strictness with which the obligation to avoid sexual relations with students must be observed. Academics must be scrupulous in their avoidance of any actions with respect to their students which will bring the academic profession into disrepute and which will damage the good name of their university among present and future students as well as before the larger public.

Teachers are often forgetful of the role which they play in affecting the future of their students. The desire to have more graduate students and assistants should not be allowed to influence the advice which teachers give to students who seek guidance about whether they should go on to work for advanced degrees. At the same time, teachers should not refuse admission to graduate students who really wish to study particular subjects and are adequately qualified even though the prospect of obtaining a satisfactory appointment in the subject is poor. A student who has reached the point of having taken a first degree, should be regarded as capable of making responsible decisions on his own.

While a teacher must respect the choices which students make on their own responsibility and with some awareness of the risks involved, the teacher must also avoid giving his blessing or encouragement to the less responsible decisions made by students. The teacher must not support students who engage in rash actions which are sometimes injurious to themselves and damaging to the university as a place of education and research. This element of the academic ethic is especially in need of emphasis in view of the conduct of many university teachers during the agitations of the 1960s and early 1970s. University teachers owe it to their students not to encourage the students' hampering of their own education, hindering the education of other students and also disrupting the conduct of research and administration. Even where the teacher is not unsympathetic with the proclaimed political objectives of the students, he must abstain from fostering the disorders of which passionate and volatile students are capable.

University teachers, particularly in the social sciences, often find it difficult to abstain from the expression of their political beliefs. Many do not attempt to do so and even say that it is impossible. Max Weber desired the exclusion of the expression of political and ethical preferences from university teaching because the relationship between teacher and students in the lecture hall rendered their criticism of his assertion unfeasible. Weber did not say that a social scientist should avoid expressing his value-judgement in seminars or in classes in which there were small numbers of students and in which they could presumably question him about his value-judgements and express their own. Weber also thought that the student should be taught "to face the facts" and this also obliged the teacher to avoid the exposition of his own political and ethical views. Teaching "the facts" as truthfully as they can be ascertained in the subject being taught would leave the student free to make his own political decisions.

It is certainly desirable that the teacher avoid exploiting the authority which is attributed to him by virtue of the fact that he has more knowledge of his subject than have his students, by expounding to them views of nature or society which are not as true as the best available techniques and the existing body of scientific and scholarly literature can sustain. It is not that a teacher in a university must suppress his own political or moral beliefs in his classes in, for example, economics, sociology, political science or any of the fields in which the subject-matter is pertinent to public controversies. But he must not claim for his assertions which touch on those subjects which are enmeshed in public controversies greater veracity than the best scientific and scholarly evidence can justify. His obligations to truthfulness should prohibit the exploitation of an audience which knows less about the subject than he does.

It must be recognised that the teacher who "sticks to the facts" might be duller than the teacher who expresses his own preferences on political and social questions. At the same time, the teacher who wishes to assert his political and social value-judgements should not spare the effort needed to make clear that he is doing so and to make as clear as he can the difference between what is supported by the most carefully assessed scientific or scholarly evidence and what is the political or moral standpoint from which he evaluates the situation. (One thing, however, is clear: the university teacher is under obligation not to use the class-room to win adherents to his own political standpoint or for his own political party.)

It is very difficult to find a plain and simple way to escape the dangers of indifference, selfishness, arbitrariness, favouritism or the imposition of extraneous beliefs. All the more urgent therefore is it to lay stress over and over again on the scruples, circumspectness and self-discipline of the individual teacher and to remind him over and over again of his obligations in teaching, examining and in other relations with his students.

The Obligations of Generations of Teachers: No academic department unless it wishes either to terminate its existence or to suffer complete discontinuity can allow itself to have most of its members of approximately the same age. In so far as individual academics participate in the making of decisions regarding academic appointments, they must bear in mind the necessity that the academic staff of the university as a whole and of each department should be spread over a wide range of ages.

The most important reason for this is that the courses offered by a department should be diversified both in subject-matter and in methods of research. Otherwise the department cannot fulfil its teaching function in relation to its field. New subject-matters and new methods in a discipline are frequently, although not always, cultivated primarily by its younger generation. A department, to say nothing of a university as a whole, which has little place in its teaching for new interests and fields and new techniques of research will do harm to the intellectual development of its students. It will also diminish its attractiveness to students and also place its graduates at a disadvantage in the competition for appointments with graduates of other universities. More important, it will handicap them in their own research because it will leave them uninstructed about the newer problems and newer techniques which emerge at the frontiers of knowledge in their respective fields.

There is another reason why heterogeneity of age is necessary. Teachers over 45 years of age often seem very old to students; they seem remote and sometimes too awe-inspiring. Under these conditions an undesirable gap can emerge between students and teachers.

Appointments committees must be very sensitive to the considerations of age in their deliberations about the merits of candidates. Often the dilemma is avoided because the post which is to be filled stipulates the rank of the appointee and this usually determines, within wide limits, the age-cohort from which the appointed candidate comes.

All this, however, is incidental to the obligations imposed by the academic ethic on teachers of different ages in their relations with each other. The relations between senior and junior members of the teaching staff now run across the entire range of academic activities—the design of a course of study, what subjects should be taught, the allocation of courses and subjects among the teachers of a department, the appointment of new staff members, the fixing of the syllabuses for the teaching of particular courses, the setting and marking of examinations, the reviews of students' achievements and problems, the allocation of prizes and studentships, the admission of new students and many others.

In every one of these categories of activities, now that they are usually no longer settled by the decision of the head of the department, the relationship between senior and junior teachers raises problems. When the departments were autocratically ruled, there were apparently no such problems since no one but the head of the department had a voice in the matter. Now, however, that there has been a dispersion of authority within departments and within the university as a whole, problems in the relations between senior members and junior members have come to the surface and must be faced.

It is not possible to deal with all of these problems or with any of them in any degree of detail. The most general consideration is the necessity for some intradepartmental consensus about the standard to be maintained in dealing with intellectual tasks. Mutual respect and trust among colleagues, regardless of their age, is one of the preconditions for the effectiveness of a department as an educational institution. The solidarity required is not merely a matter of personal friendliness among colleagues; it is also a matter of intellectual solidarity about the substance of the subjects taught and investigated and of belief in the value of the subject or discipline, but this does not entail complete unanimity about approaches and methods.

Departments usually have traditions of substantive emphasis and interests within the field which has been in their jurisdiction and they also have appropriate standards of achievement. It is important that the younger generation of teachers should be assimilated into these traditions; no less important is the provision of opportunities for the new recruits to a department to follow new approaches and to pursue the intellectual problems which they regard as most pressing.

The intellectually flexible solidarity of a department is important for the senior members and for the students but it is especially important for the younger generation of teachers who otherwise are placed in the dangerous position of being caught in a crossfire of polemics among their colleagues. Where there is conflict within and between generations, the students too often are victims of these conflicts. They become alienated from some teachers and submissive towards others and they thereby lose the benefits which are to be gained from studying with a wide range of teachers.

The traditions of departments are microcosms of the traditions of a scientific or scholarly discipline in the large. The traditions must be constantly revised and improved. Although the younger teachers and other newcomers to a department should share in them, these traditions must not be allowed to stifle the potential originality of the younger generation. The worst thing is for these younger members to feign conformity with one or another of the department's traditions while not genuinely believing in the validity of any of them.

If the intellectual traditions of a department are not kept alive and assimilated by new members the new generation of teachers will lose the intellectual benefits in what these traditions have to offer. If the existing traditions of the department are completely disregarded, the department will more easily break up into several groups, each concerned with its own sub-speciality. This is true, not only with regard to the intellectual substance of the discipline for which the department is responsible. This alienation will extend across departmental lines joining the unassimilated younger members of many departments with the result that they form a bloc within the university as a whole. If a young academic feels himself to be an outsider in his own department, he might also feel himself to be an outsider in the university as a whole. If young teachers fall into this state of mind, they will gravitate towards the discontented students and they will infuse a cynical and resentful attitude into the student body, as well as embitter themselves, and reduce their intellectual effectiveness.

The opposite alternative is also possible; the older generation of teachers in a department might conceive of themselves as being left behind intellectually, if the younger members, sometimes in association with one of the older members push the older representatives of the traditions of the department to the wall. This is a condition which is injurious to the students who are usually swept in the wake of the victorious faction in the department and who are thereby deprived of what is vital in the stock of understanding possessed by the older tradition. Still another alternative is for the older members of a department to press for the appointment to junior posts only those of the same substantive views and to refuse to allow the appointment of junior colleagues of other views. This might assure departmental solidarity but it does so at the cost of the advancement of their field of study and at the cost of their students who are prevented thereby from confronting alternative approaches in their subject.

The conditions referred to here are not only the result of personal antagonism between the older and the younger generations of teachers within any given department. They are also consequences of the development of disciplines and sub-disciplines. The introduction of new ideas is often the work of a pioneer in the older generation whose ideas are taken up and developed mainly in the younger generation. The very enthusiasm which is associated with new discoveries in a field can lead to the exaggeration of the disjunction between the new and the old and perhaps to an attitude of condescension of the exponents of the new towards those who do not follow them on their new paths.

A common responsibility of all the generations and ranks in a department and in a university is to maintain the academic ethic and the institution which it serves. It is not just a matter of "keeping the peace" within the department and within the university. Nor is it primarily a matter of treating the newly appointed younger teachers with hospitality and affection. The reason for doing these things is that they are conducive to the assimilation of the new academic generation into the academic ethic. The obligation of the longer established members must be to move them on to the path which in the course of years will make them into the co-responsible custodians of the well-being of the university as an intellectual institution.

Being loyal to one's department and being faithful to the ideals of one's discipline do not require uncritical subservience to the ideas of the reigning middle and older generations. That might maintain internal peace but it would do so at the cost of the advancement of knowledge.

Members of the older generation owe it to the ideal of the advancement of knowledge in their discipline not to be rigid in their adherence to its traditions. They owe it to their departments, to their students and to the younger generation of teachers. The responsibility lies on all sides—on the older generation not to dig their heels in to resist innovations in the field to which they have devoted their careers, on the younger generation not to act as if the ideas which their elders espoused were simply mistaken. It lies particularly on the middle generation of scientists or scholars in their forties who still have enough connections intellectually and socially with both their elders and their juniors.

For all of these reasons it is important that the younger members of a department be assimilated socially and morally into the department. This is a special responsibility of the senior and the middle-aged members of the department. The execution of this responsibility is not easy. Social incorporation and personal amiability are necessary but they are not always sufficient to eliminate dissatisfaction over the degree of equality in the conduct of departmental affairs. Some might think that there is not enough equality; others that there is too much. Yet there is bound to be a certain amount of inequality in the relations between junior and senior members of the teaching staff. These inequalities are present in many situations in which it would be wrong to attempt to eliminate them, regardless of consequences for the quality of teaching and research and for the maintenance of the university as an effective intellectual institution.

The issue of the inequality of senior and junior members of a department in the making of appointments does not arise when appointments are made by committees consisting largely of persons from outside the university or department in which the appointments are to be made. Still, even if the appointment of professors rests with mainly external appointment committees, junior appointments in these same universities are usually made by committees constituted by members of the department, elected by the department as a whole or appointed by the head of the department or by some higher authority within the university. In universities in the United States, there are seldom external appointments committees except in an advisory capacity. The appointments there are internally made or proposed.

How then are the powers of decision to be allocated among the generations or ranks in such cases? Should the lower ranks have a vote? Should they be consulted? Should young teachers in large departments have a "caucus" separate from a "senior caucus"? Should young teachers who themselves are in the department on short-term appointments and who are not yet the masters of their subject which senior members are expected to be, have an influence of equal weight with their seniors? Should those, who are committed to their university and department by long service and by the likelihood of spending the remainder of their careers there, have no more weight than those who are likely to be less committed to the university and department in consequence of the uncertainty of their future there? It is probably not advisable for junior members in short-term appointments to have a voice—or a vote—equal to that of persons who are committed to the department and the university by long service and permanent tenure.

What then should be the rights of junior members? In the case of senior appointments it is desirable that the junior members should have access to the dossiers of candidates—and that their assessments should be formally or informally solicited with a clear understanding that the confidentiality of the contents of the dossiers will be strictly observed and that their assessments will be considered seriously as advisory opinions by those who make the decision. Where the decision does not agree with the assessment of one or more of the junior members, the ground for disagreement should be explained. Perhaps the entire department should hold a preliminary, plenary discussion about the leading candidates but this discussion should not culminate in a vote by all those who participate in that discussion.

Senior members of departments should not agree to having junior members pass judgement on whether junior members who are their own colleagues and at the same time, competitors with them, should be promoted or given permanent appointments; junior members of departments should not claim this as a right. It is difficult in the egalitarian atmosphere of contemporary Western intellectual circles to exclude junior members, who are appointed on short tenure, from decisions about present and future colleagues without causing affront to them. Nevertheless their own interests are so involved that one could not be sure that the interests in their own future do not affect their assessment of the intellectual merits of their colleagues. It would also be anomalous to have persons whose stay in the university is still of uncertain duration to be given the opportunity to fix its future in a binding way.

It is felt by many nowadays to be embarrassing to argue in favour of inequality in general or in particular situations. Yet this embarrassment ought to be set aside and the junior teaching members of a department should be informed from the beginning about their responsibilities in matters of appointments. That follows from the need to make paramount the academic obligations of the department.

In decisions regarding the content of courses to be taught and the setting of examinations and marking them, there should be complete equality among teachers of different ranks. In teaching junior members should not be disproportionately burdened by routine or disesteemed tasks; they must be encouraged and enabled to do research. Concentrating routine tasks on them stands in the way of their doing research.

In the decisions as to what courses should be taught in any given year and who should teach them, the junior members should be given as much opportunity as possible to choose at least some of the courses which they will teach, in so far as this was not settled when they were appointed. At the same time, care must be taken that this arrangement does not result in the students being presented with a number of highly specialised courses which do not adequately introduce them to the subject as a whole. This imposes responsibilities on senior members as well as on junior ones. Senior members have an obligation to prevent the segregation of junior members in the teaching of elementary and unspecialised courses; senior members should regard themselves as under a shared responsibility for this type of teaching. There should also be joint courses taught by junior and senior members.

The segregation of teaching responsibilities in a way which results in junior teachers being given the responsibility for teaching introductory courses for the youngest students while senior teachers teach advanced courses for advanced students is not desirable for a number of reasons. For one thing, it prevents the junior teachers from developing their own interests in research; it also generates a belief that they are being treated as helots or as "hired hands" and hence fosters the formation of a kind of stratification within the department which is injurious to departmental solidarity. Perhaps even more important, it deprives the first-year students of the benefits of having the more comprehensive and more mature views of the subject such as are likely to be available from more experienced members of the profession, when they teach the introductory courses. If older, more senior teachers, especially those who are fairly eminent figures in their respective fields teach younger students, it heightens the students' sense of their dignity within the university as a whole. The teaching of younger students also has benefits for the more senior members of a department because it forces them to take a wider view of their subjects; if they teach only advanced students on the specialised topics on which they are doing research, they increase the always present danger that they will become so specialised that they will lose the perspective needed to appreciate fundamental issues.

Junior members should be helped by senior members to progress in their research. This flows from the dual obligation of all academics to advance knowledge as well as to transmit it. If the junior members do work together on research projects with senior members, great care must be taken that they should not be treated in the role of research assistants. Otherwise they will not learn how to stand on their own feet as investigators and they will not be stimulated to make the maximal efforts in research of which they are capable. They should be encouraged to undertake their own research and be helped in obtaining funds where funds are required. They should be very generously provided with free time, such as a term or a whole session for their research. Staff seminars and "workshops" should provide opportunities for junior members to present their research and to defend it and senior members should act in the same way. It is not desirable to allow the junior members to become isolated in their own research seminars. They need the help and the criticism of their seniors.

In all these categories of academic activity and beyond them, the senior members must avoid the peremptory exercise of their authority, which is partly official and partly an informal function of achievement. They must exercise authority; it cannot be renounced without danger to learning but it must also be done tactfully and with consideration for the dignity of those over whom it is exercised. Otherwise it is bound to arouse harsh feelings and to lead to fruitless dissension. It is very important for the work of the department and for the development of its individual members as investigators and teachers that each member of it, however junior, should have an opportunity to mature in independence, within the context of the tradition of enquiry.

To summarise: the obligation of each senior member in a department is to act in a way which will assimilate each junior member into the department and the university, to make him appreciative of its traditions and to leave him room for the development of his own intellectual individuality. The practice of a proper conviviality is among the obligations of senior members of departments, not only out of friendliness or affection but above all as an aid in the assimilation of the junior member to the academic ethic in general as well as into the particular department and the particular university.

It is pertinent at this point to say something about the obligations of junior teachers. It is important that they should not give such primacy to their research that it leads them to neglect their teaching. It is also important that they should regard themselves as members of their departments and of their university, even though their tenure is of uncertain duration, and take seriously any administrative duties which fall to their lot. It is not easy, in a period when many senior academics have allowed, or even aided, the disaggregation of their universities, for the new generation of teachers to develop a sense of the university as a corporate body collectively engaged in intellectual work. Nevertheless junior teachers are under obligation, if they envisage an academic career for themselves, to become aware that they must share in the collective responsibility for their respective universities as well as for their own departments. They must see that their departments and their universities are more than administrative conveniences and sources of funds and services. They should be willing to allow themselves to be drawn into the life and spirit of their universities.

Obligations of Colleagues: (i) The relationship among colleagues in a university is first of all a relationship within a department. It is also a relationship with colleagues in substantively neighbouring departments; it is also a relationship with colleagues scattered throughout the university, and the universities elsewhere in the country and abroad.

Since it is desirable that a department should offer to its students and the learned world a variety of established and new lines of interpretation and techniques, it must be accepted that an entire department should not be of a single intellectual stamp. Just as it is not good for the students to learn only one part of a field, only one approach to it, only one set of techniques for studying it, and only one theory for interpreting it, so it is not good for colleagues to be surrounded by a homogeneous intellectual environment. But even where there is general agreement about approaches, techniques and theories within a department, there are still bound to be disagreements. Some of these disagreements will be intellectual, some of them will be an outcome of uncongenial temperaments, or of disagreements about academic and public policy. There are also bound to be disagreements between colleagues in a department about the merits of candidates for appointment and promotion, about the content of courses and the like. All these academic disagreements are quite legitimate and even desirable but they should be conducted in a restrained manner by those who are parties to them.

Senior academics have an obligation to contain both those disagreements in which they participate and those disagreements among their departmental colleagues to which they are witnesses. They should try as hard as they can to "purify" their own and their colleagues' disagreements so that they are disagreements about purely academic matters, and to exclude or suppress such disagreements as derive purely and simply from their own personal, temperamental, political and other extraneous considerations. This calls for restraint by each person on his own expression of such tendencies and his resistance to allowing himself to be drawn by the expression of such tendencies in others. These are obligations of civility, respect and courtesy within one's own university and beyond. It is contrary to the obligations to colleagues to disparage them before students or in public. It is perfectly within the boundaries of academic citizenship to criticise the work of colleagues in writing or orally before peers or students; personal vilification is not within those boundaries.

The head or convenor of the department or faculty must play a major role in trying to keep an amiable peace among its disagreeing members. He can do this by evenhandedness and patience in meetings and by trying to reconcile individuals in conflict with each other by talking with them individually. Without solidarity, mutual trust and mutual respect among the senior members of the department, the junior members, worried about their own future in the department, will become partisans. The chairman must avoid giving the impression that he is in the hands of a clique or of one powerful personality in the department. Confidentiality will be broken in the search for allies and rumours of conflict will spread among junior teachers and from them to students, with resulting fears on the part of the young members—teachers and graduate students—about being on the wrong side. Cynicism about the department and the discipline among the students will result.

Relations with colleagues in other departments or faculties should be fostered for the intellectual benefit that might accrue since important new problems are often to be found at the boundaries of disciplines, and also so that the university should form a coherent corporate body and not be simply a convenient administrative context for the pursuit by each individual of his own specialised intellectual interests. The cultivation of friendly relations with colleagues in adjacent departments is an obligation on all members, senior and junior. Wherever possible and appropriate, courses should be given jointly by members of different departments and joint appointments in several departments should be sympathetically considered.

Opportunities should be taken and arrangements made for members of different departments to meet informally, to become aware of each other, to become aware of the intellectual problems they face in teaching and research and which are of significance beyond the boundaries of individual departments. The quality of a university can be benefited by the concern of its teaching staff about the standing of the university as a whole, as well as about the quality or intellectual achievement of particular departments other than their own. A university needs an "invisible senate", a stiffening spine which, outside the formal and official committees and boards, spreads its concern for the university beyond the boundaries of departments and up to the boundaries of the university. This "invisible senate" cannot be planned; it must emerge from the relationship of colleagues throughout the university. It arises from a sense of obligation to the university as an intellectual institution. This is not the same as being an "academic politician"; it means acting in a patently disinterested manner in a way which gains the general acknowledgement of colleagues.

Good relations with colleagues in other universities should be maintained. This is necessary for the benefit of each particular discipline. It is also desirable for the purpose of promoting the solidarity of the academic community as a whole within particular countries and across national boundaries. The republic of learning runs beyond national boundaries and its maintenance and prosperity should be one of the concerns of those who are committed to the academic ethic. Jealousy and disparagement of other institutions, regardless of whether they are of approximately the same rank of eminence or higher or lower, should be avoided.

Some differences in the status of individual universities is inevitable. It is important, however, that this differentiation not be allowed to enter into the relations of colleagues. In countries in which universities are dispersed over a wide range of eminence in terms of scientific and scholarly achievements, age, location, wealth, quality of students attracted, etc., the problem of the relations between universities higher in the hierarchy of deference and those which are lower emerges.

It is important that persons who teach in the less eminent universities should not become discouraged because their universities are not so highly regarded by the outside world. The tasks of teaching and research are just as incumbent on members of less famous universities as they are on members of more famous ones. The tasks of academic citizenship are urgent in all universities, both the famous ones and the obscure ones.

(ii) One of the obligations of every teacher and of everyone who does scientific or scholarly research is to scrutinise the tradition of his subject, to winnow out the valid and important from the invalid and unimportant. This must be done both in teaching and research. The critical scrutiny of the tradition and particularly of the most recent increments to it is an obligation of a university teacher to his colleagues in his own university and at others, present and future, even where it requires that he render negative judgements on their work.

This obligation is also performed through reviewing recently published treatises and monographs in scientific and scholarly journals partly in the form of book reviews, for which ordinarily no monetary remuneration is received, and partly in the form of "reviews of the literature". The relative importance of these two forms of the assessment of recent literature in any field varies from one field to the other. In the natural sciences, the "review of the literature" is more important than book reviews; the reverse is probably the case in the humanistic and social science disciplines.

Book reviews and "reviews of the literature" are indispensable parts of the institutional machinery of learning. They not only inform colleagues of the existence of books, monographs and papers which they might otherwise not learn about—at least not for a long time—but they sort the wheat from the chaff. More than that, they even improve the wheat by critical comments, supplementations and corrections. Book-reviewing and the writing of reviews of the literature are onerous tasks; to do them properly requires hard work. Yet, it is in many fields very painstakingly done. Indeed it is a testimonial to the strength of the academic and scientific ethos that scientists and scholars who have so much else to do, go to such trouble and spend so much time to serve their colleagues with minimal financial remuneration, if any, and not very much glory. There are also fields in which the standard of reviewing is not so high. In such fields it behoves editors of journals to try to raise the standard by instructions to invited reviewers and by greater care in the selection of reviewers.

At an earlier stage in the process of serving professional colleagues through improving the intellectual tradition of a subject is the reviewing of manuscripts which have been submitted for publication, either as papers in journals or as books and monographs. Whatever the "average level of quality" of published papers and books in any given field, it is undoubtedly higher than the "average level" of what has been submitted for publication. This first winnowing relies upon the readiness of university teachers to devote some of their time and energy to the burdensome task of "refereeing" papers, writing specific criticisms of them, and often, numerous and lengthy suggestions for revision and improvement. Much that sees the light of publication has been rendered fit for entry into that state by the careful and self-sacrificing—also financially unremunerated—work of referees and editors.

It is the same with respect to the publication of books and monographs by commercial and academic publishing firms. Here university teachers do not possess such exclusive responsibility for the quality of what is published as they do in the publication of scientific and scholarly journals. They have to share their influence with publishers' editors, who are often inexpert in the subjects dealt with and directors of firms who have to consider commercial profitability, the prestige of the firm and other factors which are not always closely correlated with scientific or scholarly merit. Nevertheless the academics' obligation should be unaffected by these non-academic considerations.

Another service to colleagues is the critical reading of manuscripts of other academics prior to submission for publication. Although each scientist and scholar bears the full responsibility for whatever he publishes, he often requests a colleague in his own field to read his manuscript and to recommend improvements. To do this well is a time-consuming work but whoever is asked to do so and who agrees to do it owes it to his subject as well as to his colleagues to do so as stringently as he can. It is an equal obligation of the person who makes the request to take seriously the criticism and suggestions made by the colleague who has read the manuscript.

(iii) One of the assumptions of the academic ethic is mutuality in the exchange of knowledge among colleagues. The open publication of the results of research is not only an obligation on university teachers; it is also a right which university teachers are entitled to expect from their colleagues. The asymmetry of secretiveness on one side and openness on the other is an infringement of the academic ethic. This raises the question of how those who are knowingly committed to and observant of the academic ethic should conduct themselves towards university teachers who do not adhere to that ethic.

Some special problems arise regarding the secrecy of research which is done with the financial support of governments or private business firms.

The general obligation of openness is contradicted by the obligation of secrecy. Should a scientist who has done research for a governmental institution which desires that a particular paper should not be published agree to meet that request? Should an academic scientist agree to disclose the results of his research before they are published, to a foreign colleague who will convey that knowledge to a governmental body or private firm in his own country which will in turn use it to place his country in a position of military or commercial advantage over the country of the scientist who has done the research? Should an academic scientist serve as a consultant to a government or to a private firm on scientific matters which are to be kept secret?

As to whether an academic scientist who has, with governmental financial support, produced a particular paper which the governmental body support-ing the research wishes to have withheld from publication, should agree to the withholding, is a matter which the individual and the governmental body in question should decide between themselves in each case. If all of the results of the scientist's research emerging from the particular project are to be kept secret, then he should not seek to do that kind of research in his capacity as a member of a university. If the problem arises only occasionally, no major difficulty arises.

With regard to the question of whether an academic scientist should refuse to allow a foreign colleague of good credentials to know the results of his research before they are published, there is little harm in such disclosure prior to publication if the results are going in any case to be published. The loss of technological advantage to a competing country occurs less through the publication of scientific research than through the commercial sale of equipment embodying the technological innovation. Control over this kind of loss should be done, if it is to be done at all, by governments or private firms or both in collaboration; it is not something for individual academics to attempt on their own.

On the question whether an academic scientist should provide consulta-tive services to a government or a private firm regarding scientific matters which must be kept secret, there is no problem at all if the consultation does not require that the research of the consultant-scientist be kept secret and if the consultative services do not intrude into the performance of the scientist's primary obligation of teaching, research and academic citizenship. It would be contrary to the academic ethic if the scientist in question spent most of his time in the provision of such consultative services at the cost of his research and teaching, just as it would be if all of his research was classified as secret. But if he spends only about one day weekly on such services, no problem would seem to be raised.

The principle is clear: research done by academic scientists and scholars should be made available to their academic colleagues within their own country and in other countries. Free communications of the results of research is one of the conditions of the advancement of knowledge. Exceptions to this principle should be decided from case to case, with the burden of proof lying on those who desire the exception.

The Obligations of University Teachers in Academic Appointments: The extent of adherence to the criterion of achievement in teaching and research in matters of academic appointment affects the quality of a university. It is true that the intellectual intensity of the internal life of a university does indeed affect the quality of the performance of its teachers but even universities of the highest quality cannot make silk purses out of sows' ears. A poor university can ruin a good or promising scientist or scholar; a good one can induce a good scientist or scholar to exert himself up to the level of his potentiality; it can induce him to extend himself. But the talent and the intellectual passion must be there already, although sometimes hidden from a casual eye. The task of every appointive committee is to seek out these qualities in the candidates whom it has invited or who have been called to its attention by application or recommendation. Its task then is to choose the intellectually best person who can be appointed, given the salary available and the prestige of the university.

It is the high quality of achievement and no less the sense of the imperative of high quality of achievement which gives to a good university the tone which brings out the best in its teaching and research and which communicates itself to its students. Mutual trust, mutual respect, solicitousness for younger members and the like are all indispensable but they cannot compensate for the absence of rigour in the choice of new members for the academic staff of a university; the decisions to discontinue, re-appoint or promote persons already appointed must apply the same standards as are appropriate to the appointment of new members.

How are appointments to be made? The net must be widely cast. In countries where academic appointments are advertised, appointments committees should not regard themselves as confined to the consideration only of persons who propose themselves. They must look over the whole field, as well as they can survey it, on the basis of their knowledge of the published literature and recommendations by qualified persons. They must study the writings, published and unpublished, of those who are willing to be candidates and they must interview those whom they consider seriously. They should never think of merely filling a post on permanent appointment because one is vacant; if there is no candidate of the calibre which they think the salary, status, privileges and resources which their university offers should attract, they should leave the post unfilled. Short-term appointments which may be extended to permanent appointments should be made by the same standards as permanent appointments. Incumbency should not be one of the criteria of re-appointment or promotion. Necessary and routine teaching for which no already appointed member is available, can be done by rigorously delimited temporary appointments, which should be kept temporary, until a person worthy of a regular appointment can be found.

Every promotion from a post on short tenure to one on permanent or long tenure should be treated as a new appointment; the whole field should be scanned to see, whether, for the salary, opportunities and resources to be provided for the post, the candidate for promotion is the best possible person available in the country, or internationally, at the time. If he is not, his promotion should be refused and a better person appointed in his stead. Friendship and personal familiarity must be relentlessly and absolutely resisted as criteria of appointment.

It is difficult to assess teaching which one has not observed over an extended period, or experienced as a pupil and reflected on in later years, but an assessment of teaching ability must nonetheless be made. Distinction in research is somewhat easier to assess since its results are public but that is not easy either. External referees should be consulted but their testimonials should be taken with a grain of salt because external referees are often generous at the expense of a university which is not their own. National origin, race, colour, friendship, sex, religion, politics and personal charm must be completely excluded from consideration as irrelevant to the teacher's task. The chosen candidate must also be a person who will do his duty to the university and the academic world as a loyal and responsible academic citizen, but a disposition to "rock the boat" must be disregarded if it is compensated by high quality of teaching and research. A person of outstanding intellectual qualities in teaching and research who is inclined to "rock the boat" from vanity or selfishness or the sheer pleasure of being a bull in a china shop, should be told, if he is invited to take up an appointment that he will be expected to behave himself in a gentlemanly way with due consideration for his colleagues. This might be difficult to do but it might sometimes be necessary. Academic citizenship should be considered together with proficiency in teaching and research.

Fifty years ago, it would not have been necessary to stipulate the adduction of the criterion of academic citizenship. After the experience of the 1960s and the 1970s, it is now necessary to consider it explicitly. Does the candidate believe in the possibility of the disinterested pursuit of truth, however tentatively that truth is to be held and asserted? Does he believe that academic freedom is the freedom of an academic to place political ends above intellectual ends in the university? Does he believe that the proper end of teaching is to win the student for a particular political party or movement? Obviously, questions like these cannot be asked directly or in as simple a form as they have just been put but the implicit or explicit answer to such questions are things that members of an appointment committee must take into account in assessing the fitness of a candidate for an appointment to a university.

This emphasis on academic citizenship is not intended to supersede or subordinate devotion to teaching and to discovery. But since under modern conditions nearly all advanced teaching and a great deal of basic research take place predominantly in universities, the disordering of universities damages both teaching and research. The politicisation of universities by those who believe in the primacy of politics everywhere, including universities, is a menace to the intellectual efficacy of universities. It is inimical to disciplined learning, to teaching, study and research.

A Note on Pluralism: It is appropriate at this point to insert some observations about "pluralism" or, as it has come to be called in recent years, "pluralism of standpoints". In universities 50 years ago, when there was one professor in a department, it was the professor's conception of the scope of the subject, the basic ideas and the most appropriate techniques that prevailed. Nowadays, in many universities, there are numerous professors in many departments and departments tend to have numerous members, with a fairly large proportion in the higher ranks. The uniformity of definition and outlook characteristic of the older type of department is no longer necessary or acceptable. For one thing, many disciplines include many sub-specialities. There are also different views about the relative importance of particular problems, about interpretations of certain phenomena and about the best methods of investigation. It is obvious that any department which wishes to educate its students adequately must do justice to these legitimate differences in approach towards scientific and scholarly matters. It must also maintain a certain catholicity with respect to the constituent specialities, although it is not incumbent in every department to cover all the fields of specialisation.

In the past 15 years, there has emerged a demand for "pluralism of standpoints". This demand for pluralism is usually not for the substantive and technical heterogeneity of the various disciplines, although it sometimes speaks in that idiom. It is rather a demand for the academic establishment of a particular political standpoint, usually Marxism, in one or more of its recent variant forms. Under the guise of "methodological pluralism" or the "pluralism of paradigms", the argument for the "pluralism of standpoints" is frequently an argument for the appointment of Marxists.

Marxism is, of course, a prominent political programme and it has in the course of time also developed a fairly large body of literature, some of which is substantive, and much of which is doctrinal polemic. Since it is important to avoid political criteria in appointments and to avoid political propaganda in teaching, this kind of pluralism must be viewed very sceptically. It would be a serious disservice to higher learning to allow political criteria to be used in the appointment and promotion of staff-members. At the same time, substantive and technical diversity within a department must be carefully nurtured.

What is wanted is intellectual diversity, the diversity of legitimate standpoints of objects, methods and interpretation, within the various scientific and scholarly fields. It is difficult sometimes to see clearly a boundary line between legitimate and illegitimate diversity. It is not possible to promulgate a criterion in formal terms—but this is like much else in life. Nevertheless, good-will, conscientious reflection on experience and knowledge of the subject-matter allow reasonable judgement.

In any case, arguments for the representation of political standpoints must not be given countenance, regardless of whether the political standpoint is liberal, radical or conservative, revolutionary, moderate or reactionary. No person should be excluded from consideration because of his political standpoint; no person should be preferred because of his political standpoint.

Academics have an obligation to respect the confidentiality of deliberations regarding appointments. The disclosure to the press, or to the persons whose appointments have been discussed or to other persons, of the details of the deliberations of appointive bodies or of the testimonials submitted to them, and particularly to disclose how the individual members of the committee voted is an infringement on the obligation of confidentiality.

In matters of appointment academics play an important part as referees regarding candidates for appointment in other universities. It is part of the obligation of a teacher to write to prospective employers about his former and present students or colleagues when they seek to obtain appointments in universities, private business, research institutions and governments or when they are applying for research grants, graduate studentships, assistant-ships or research fellowships. This is a demanding and unceasing obligation of university teachers. University teachers are also often requested to assess the work of a person who has been neither their immediate colleague nor their student and who is being considered for appointment at another university.

Of course the letters of referees are not decisive but they are certainly often taken into account. One of the reasons why they are not taken into account as much as they might be is that the members of the appointment committee to whom they are addressed often distrust them. Although they have usually been solicited, those who have solicited them may suspect that they exaggerate the merits of the particular candidate about whom they have been written. The referees themselves are often in a false position. They write on behalf of a former student whom they wish to help to make his way academically; they also wish to tell the truth but they fear that the candidate on behalf of whom they are writing will be at a disadvantage if his faults are described as well as his virtues because they believe that the other referees will mention only the merits of their candidates and will even exaggerate them. For this reason, a very useful mode of advisory assessment is rendered unreliable and even useless. This is especially the case where the candidate is just at the beginning of his career and his referee wants to help him to get started. (In the United States, the dilemma is especially acute since the confidentiality of the referees' letters cannot be guaranteed.)

There is no simple solution to this vicious circle of inflation of testimonials. As in other situations, a more widespread probity is necessary.

Note on the Right to Participate in Decisions regarding Appointments: Any discussion about the obligation of members of appointment committees must face the problems raised by earlier negligence, light-heartedness, sheer mistakes, or the failure of a well-chosen candidate to realise his promise. It is obvious in every university that some departments are weaker than their past standing, the resources available and the standing of the university as a whole justify. Vigilance over new appointments cannot undo past errors in appointment, except over a long period. But even this curative vigilance is unlikely, if the departments which are the victims of those errors and faults have the power of appointment, with only perfunctory scrutiny of its recommendations by the higher authorities of the university. In that case, the result will be self-perpetuation, at the same level of mediocrity, through the appointment of their own former pupils and friends and other persons of indifferent qualities. The question may be put as follows: are members of weak departments entitled to the privilege of selecting or recommending for appointment their new members?

Academics who have been careless in the application of stringent criteria of achievement in making or recommending appointments are not entitled to participate in decisions regarding appointments. For this reason academics should recognise the appropriateness of a governing body or officer of the university to suspend a weak department's right to propose appointments. This procedure is applicable mainly in universities in which appointive decisions or recommendations rest substantially with departments or committees made up of members of the department to which the appointment is to be made. Such arrangements obtain chiefly in the United States but even in countries where the final decision is made by government officials in ministries of education, the power of recommendation is usually in the hands of the department or faculty to which the appointment is to be made. The situation is somewhat different when the power of appointment or of recommendation lies with committees for professorial appointments made up largely of external members, and the proposals made here do not apply.

It would take much courage on the part of the university teachers and administrators to restrict a department's or a faculty's power of appointment in a university where the tradition of departmental or faculty autonomy is well established. It could only be done where the governing bodies and the influential members of the teaching staffs are alert to the damage which poor appointments do to the intellectual quality of the university and if academic citizenship is stronger than the desire to let sleeping dogs lie.

Note on Permanent Tenure: Permanent or indefinite tenure is one of the major objects of the decisions of appointments committees. It has been generally accepted that senior academics should be appointed on permanent—or indefinite—tenure and the attainment of that state is a crucial feature of the academic career. An academic who has attained permanent tenure is genuinely regarded as having "arrived". It is worthwhile to enquire into the question of whether permanent tenure is desirable in the light of its consequences for the adequate fulfilment of the obligations of the academic profession.

There is no clear reason why academics alone in the world should claim permanence of tenure without the possibility of removal. Even the Roman Catholic Church can defrock a priest. Why should the universities, which have taken the pattern of permanence of tenure from the church and more immediately in some countries from the civil service, retain a teacher permanently when he has clearly been unfaithful to the unspoken commitment which he has undertaken on entry into the academic career? Furthermore, why should an academic who has become indolent and negligent about his obligations in teaching, and who does no research or who does poor research be guaranteed security? A teacher who is frivolous in matters of academic citizenship may, if he has permanent tenure, be so with the confidence that nothing can be done to terminate his appointment. Permanent tenure can turn an academic post into a sinecure with rights and without obligations.

Why in the first place, should university teachers be appointed with the assurance that they are guaranteed incumbency until the age of retirement? One of the main arguments for permanence of tenure is that it protects the academic from the menace of dismissal as a sanction for the independent expression of politically and intellectually heterodox views. Permanence of tenure allows an individual scientist or scholar to embark on potentially important investigations which might run over many years and which might not yield results until a long time has passed. The need for short-term investigations of less importance in order to demonstrate that the person is worthy of reappointment is reduced by permanent appointment. These are strong arguments for permanent tenure.

There are other good arguments for the maintenance of the institution of appointment on "permanent tenure". One of the consequences of "permanent tenure" is that it holds in check the noxious effects of the extent of mobility. A teacher appointed on permanent tenure in a particular university is more likely to regard the university as the institution in which he will probably spend the rest of his career. He is more likely therefore to be concerned about its well-being and its good name for achievement in teaching and research. That this does not always happen is quite evident but it is equally evident that it does happen in many cases. The elimination of permanent tenure would increase the amount of movement between universities, partly because the appointments of many more persons would be discontinued and partly because many more individuals would seek appointments elsewhere if they were not assured that they could remain indefinitely where they are. A university depends for its intellectual well-being, in some measure, on its "invisible senate" which is made up of teachers who are concerned with more than their own scientific and scholarly achievements, their own teaching and their own departments. Such individuals who are at best a small minority within any university would probably become fewer and the smaller number might be less influential if permanent tenure were to be eliminated.

It is also possible that, since the elimination of permanent tenure would entail periodic review and deliberation about the merits and deficiencies of every member of the academic staff, it would entail either an immense addition to the work of all colleagues who were called upon to assess the achievements of the colleague under review, or it would be done in a perfunctory and slipshod way. It might result in "log-rolling" and in the formation of cliques and factions made of persons who support each other in the periodic assessments. As a result of the elimination of permanent tenure, conflicts and divisions might become even more common than they are at present.

If permanent tenure were eliminated it is certainly possible that indolence would be reduced. So its critics assert. Academics might under the threat of the discontinuance of their appointments be more conscientious in their teaching; it is also likely that more of them who do little research and who publish little under conditions of permanent tenure would do more research and publish more papers. The latter outcome would be a very doubtful blessing. Research conceived and conducted under the threat of the loss of an appointment is not likely to be inspired by intellectual curiosity; it would probably be rather humdrum work of which there is too much already.

Thus although the present arrangements for permanent tenure do give rise to abuses, it is not certain that the alternative scheme of periodic reassessment and reappointment or dismissal would not have equally injurious consequences for the realisation of the idea of the university as an institution of research and teaching at a high level. This does not mean that the present system might not be modified with advantages to the academic ethic.

The Obligations and Interests of University Teachers: "Interests" are prospective advantages or benefits which would accrue to individuals and groups under certain conditions. These benefits are usually understood as pecuniary benefits and physical conveniences. Members of the academic profession like all other members of society have interests. They are interested in having the highest possible salaries, the most congenial working conditions, the shortest working week, etc. How are these interests to be dealt with in the light of the obligations of the academic profession? "Interests" are often in conflict with obligations. Should interests override obligations? Should obligations override interests? Is there always a conflict between obligations and interests, and if there is, how can a way be found which assuages this conflict?

There is no necessary incompatibility with the academic ethic if university teachers, through an organisation, negotiate about their salaries, conditions of work, insurance benefits, etc., with a national body which determines academic salaries. It may be argued that there is no infringement on the academic ethic, if university teachers, through their representatives, bargain as a trade union with the administration of their university regarding their salaries, conditions of work, pensions and insurance benefits, etc. If it is done in a matter-of-fact way, and if the bargaining is about classes or ranks of persons, there need be nothing injurious in this. Nevertheless, the formation of a trade union of university teachers and its proceeding in the style of ordinary unions raises grave questions for the ethos of the academic profession.

If decisions about reappointment, promotions and the granting of permanent tenure of individuals are made into objects of negotiations by trade unions with academic administrators and if incumbency and seniority are to be made into criteria of appointment—and more especially of reappointment and promotion—damage will be done to the particular university in which it occurs and in the course of time to universities in general and to the progress of learning. If permanent tenure and automatic promotion may be presumed for all academics who are represented by trade unions, the selection which is necessary for creating, maintaining and rewarding the highest levels of achievement in the leading universities—and not only in those—will be brought to an end. Every university will be condemned to live with the inevitable errors of its earlier decisions in matters of appointment.

There is another danger which the formation of academic trade unions brings to the maintenance of the solidarity of the academic staff formed around their own particular university and around the idea of the university in general.

If the trade union movement among university teachers takes the form which it has taken in the working class, it will harden the lines of cleavage in a dichotomised university, split between "we", the academic staff, and "they", the administrators. This is already an obstacle to the formation of corporate solidarity around intellectual values in universities.

Academics in Great Britain and in Israel have joined trade unions, which in their negotiations with their respective national ministries, have confined themselves to salary-scales. There is a danger, which is however not inevitable, that academic trade unions will exceed this self-restriction. If the restriction to matters of salary-scales is exceeded and the trade union unit within the university becomes a focus of loyalty, attachment to the idea of the university and to the particular university as a corporate entity concentrated on the pursuit and transmission of truth about serious things, will be injured.

It is perfectly reasonable for the custodial staffs of universities, the electricians, plumbers, janitors and other manual workers who are necessary to the maintenance of the physical plant of the university to join trade unions to improve their wages and conditions of work in the same way that workers in factories and offices do in liberal-democratic countries. Trade unions have generally not been concerned with the relative merits of the performance of individuals, they have traditionally been concerned to deflect attention from individually distinctive excellence and to conduct their arguments on behalf of comprehensive categories such as all the workers in a given plant or industry and in a given occupation. The aspirations of academic trade unions and the obligations of university teachers in matters of academic appointments are in principle antithetical to each other.

(It is also contradictory for university teachers to claim that they are employees under the authority of others and at the same time to assert that they have a right to share in the exercise of authority by the corporate bodies which govern the university and its subsidiary faculties and departments, but this is of secondary importance.)

There are several reasons why trade unions of the traditional sort are inappropriate to universities. The first is that in a university, there is no equivalent to the profit-seeking or profit-making employers whose profit depends in part on how little or much he must pay to his employees. The second and more important reason is that the idea of the free labour market in which the possessors of labour power "sell" their labour power to the higher bidder, does not rest well with the idea of the university where teachers, although they must gain their livelihood as teachers, are in principle concerned with the acquisition of truth through research and with the transmission to students and colleagues of truths discovered by themselves and others. The establishment of a "closed shop" which makes the holding of an academic appointment dependent on membership in the trade union adds another obstacle to the strict application of academic criteria in decisions regarding appointments.

In the United States and to a smaller extent in Western Germany, there are, at the time of appointment, negotiations between individual teachers and heads of departments or administrative officers about salaries and certain conditions of work but in these cases, it is a matter of what the university authorities are willing to pay to a particular individual teacher, bearing in mind his standing as a scientist or scholar and as a teacher. Academic criteria are clearly involved. This is not the case in trade union negotiations about salary scales which are uniform for all persons within the given institution or system, and within particular ranks and grades of seniority. Trade union representations about the cases of individual university teachers, in the countries where the academic traditions concern themselves with individuals, seldom concern themselves with the intellectual and pedagogical achievements of the individuals. It is perhaps true that representations by trade unions or staff associations do serve to protect individual teachers from unfair discrimination or dismissal but questions of intellectual merit seldom are raised in such cases; at best it is contended that the minimal requirements of performance have been met or that the proper administrative procedures have not been followed in dealing with the individual in question.

These observations regarding academic trade unions need to be supplemented by the observation that the deleterious potentialities of trade unions for the functioning of the university as an intellectual institution are exacerbated when the academic trade union has a definite political cast and when it attempts to influence new appointments as well as reappointments and promotions of particular individuals.

Still, the fact of the unionisation of university teachers remains and it is not likely to disappear, although for the moment the tide has ceased to rise—at least in the United States. It is necessary to affirm the obligation of academics who adhere to trade unions to support only negotiations about salary-scales and to abstain from intervening in cases of the appointment, promotion and discontinuance of individual teachers except in cases of patent procedural irregularities. Once a trade union becomes the rectifier of individual "grievances", it is likely to introduce extra-intellectual criteria for the determination of whether particular individuals should be appointed, reappointed, or granted promotion or permanent tenure. If the trade union presumes to deal with individual cases, it will tend to encroach upon the jurisdiction of appointive bodies which are intended to apply strictly academic criteria. By its very nature as a trade union, it is likely to try to obtain maximum security for its members, *i.e.*, permanence of tenure from initial appointment onward. If the trade union of university teachers undertakes to define criteria to govern reappointment, promotion and the granting of permanent tenure, it is likely to argue for criteria which will be antithetical to the criteria of intellectual excellence in teaching, research and academic citizenship.

The Obligation to their own University: University teachers owe obligations to the particular institutions in which they are holding appointments. This obligation is not a composite of obligations to their students and their colleagues. There is an obligation to sustain the particular university because it is a source of intellectual sustenance to its members. A university is of intellectual importance to its members through the immediate and specific stimulation of a new idea suggested or expounded by a colleague and through the critical and sympathetic response of a colleague or a student to an idea put forward by the individual teacher. But it also has an important intellectual function in presenting an environment of high standards of intellectual exertion and achievement. This environment of many intellec-tually active individuals is also fused into an anonymous, collective representative of the standards of intellectual activity. It is a constant reminder of the urgency of searching, studying, criticising, re-examining old texts and data, seeking new data and putting them together with the old data. A university, in addition to its tangible, physical reality is a collectivity which stands over, in an impersonal way, all of its members who are sensitive to it. The university is an intellectual collectivity, and not just a collection of stimulating individuals and necessary services provided by the university; it is not just a legal construct and it is not an epiphenomenon. It is a general pattern of attitudes and activities which moulds the activities of the individual members of the university. If this pattern is dissipated, it has a debilitating effect on the relation of teachers and students and of colleagues and colleagues. It is a pattern which is sustained by academic citizenship. By his own exertions, achievements and bearing, each individual adds his own force to the strengthening of that impersonal intellectual collectivity, making it more apprehensible and more present to colleagues and pupils, present and future.

In addition to this strengthening of the university as an intellectual collectivity, there is a need to make it match the pride which those associated with it would like to have in it. Pride in an institution is not just the gratification drawn from its fame, from the esteem in which its accomplishments are held in the society outside the university. Individual academics are proud of their university when they see it as embodying the virtues espoused in the academic ethic. A university does not have to be the greatest university in the world in order for its members to be proud of it. Pride is, of course, sustained by achievement but not all achievement consists in the publication of ground-breaking scientific and scholarly papers and monographs or educating students who become Nobel Prize-laureates or professors in leading universities. Pride in a university is a function of affectionate attachment to it and of its respect for the obligations of the academic ethic. This is quite compatible with interest in and responsiveness to the demand and standards of the larger community of scientists or scholars in the teacher's own field of special concentration far beyond the boundaries of any single university. Loyalty to the latter does not necessitate indifference towards the particular university in which an individual holds his appointment.

The good name of a particular university among other universities and in society at large maintains pride in the university and makes for its effectiveness as an intellectual environment. This is why university teachers have an obligation to do nothing which will bring their university into the contumely of the academic and the larger worlds by dishonourable conduct or frivolity or by pushing it into the infringement of the academic ethic.

In a university, there are very likely to be conflicts about intellectual matters; there may also be conflicts over individual status and the status of departments and groups of departments about the allocations of resources and of influence within the university. The conflicts over intellectual matters not infrequently also become conflicts about non-intellectual matters. Not all conflicts in universities are conflicts over intellectual differences although these conflicts over the exercise of power and resources are often put forward as intellectual conflicts. Whereas intellectual conflicts especially if conducted in a reasonable tone can be very fruitful for the growth of knowledge, the conflicts over power and resources are seldom helpful either intellectually or institutionally.

The obligation to one's university includes the obligation to try to check conflicts within the university, between the representatives of disciplines and of sets of disciplines, between individuals and between factions, between groups of students and groups of teachers and between teachers and administrators. It is one of the vices of large universities—but not always confined to them—to foster animosity of teachers towards administrators, especially when they are full-time administrators, who are regarded as "they" in contrast to "we", the teachers. In universities where there were few full-time administrators, and where the higher administrators returned to their academic duties after limited periods of services as deans, rectors and provosts, this was not such an acute issue because "they" were drawn from and returned to "us". In the very large universities of the type of which not so many existed before the Second World War and of which many came into existence after it, administrators became professional administrators to an increasing extent. This occurred even on the continent of Europe and in Great Britain. A large full-time administrative bureaucracy was a longer-established arrangement in the United States, and it has become larger since the Second World War. This administrative development has brought with it frictions and dissatisfactions with "their" actions. This, together with disciplinary boundaries and sub-disciplinary specialisation, the increased political interest and partisanship, and disappointment connected with failure to progress within the academic profession, have led to distrust—even hostility—not only towards the administration but towards "the university".

Severe cleavages between academics and their administrators weaken the academic ethos. They distract attention from teaching and research. They destroy the serenity and concentration of mind needed in universities. They precipitate and aggravate conflicts when there are political disorders within and outside the university and when the solidarity of the university should be reaffirmed.

It is right that the cleavage between university teachers and administrators should be diminished. It demands forbearance, patience and the avoidance of arbitrariness on the part of both the academics and the administrators. An understanding of the necessities of the university as a whole is the minimal obligation of all individual academics; a respect for the requirements of courtesy, openness and fair dealing with teachers and students is the minimal obligation of administrators.

Regardless of whether a university is a wholly self-governing and internally relatively "democratic" institution, much of the work of maintaining a university, apart from the actual performance of teaching and scientific and scholarly research and the details of administration is done by committees. The committees are almost invariably advisory to some higher authority in the university, whether that authority is the president or vice-chancellor, or rector, dean or chairman of a faculty or a faculty board or of a department or a department as a whole. Conscientious service on committees has become proportionately more necessary as universities have increased in size. Much that was previously accomplished in an informal manner has now to be done through formally called and conducted meetings.

Membership of committees is a burden except for those who have lost interest in the intellectual substance of academic life or who enjoy them as occasions for the struggle for power; such membership is in many ways a distraction for individual academics from the central tasks of teaching and research. Committees proliferate, unfortunately, sometimes fruitlessly, and much time can be taken up by them. They are also often very trying and tiresome because some of their members talk too much and because the chairman cannot keep control over the proceedings. Nevertheless, service on committees, and above all, the chairmanship of committees is indispensable to the government of a university as a corporate entity and as an intellectual collectivity. Unfortunately, it is often the best members of a university, those most fully imbued with its ethic and most outstanding in their intellectual achievements who lose patience with the increase of work in committees. The belief that the reports of committees are disregarded by those to whom they are submitted is further discouragement to serious participants. One result of these views is that committees are left to "professional committee-men" whose interests are often not primarily academic. Academics have an obligation to prevent this from happening by accepting their responsibility for service on committees and by increasing the efficiency of committees.

THE OBLIGATIONS OF THE ACADEMIC PROFESSION
TO ITS ENVIRONING SOCIETY

Universities have dual obligations. On the one side, they are responsible for the maintenance and advancement of knowledge and on the other they are responsible for performing important functions for their societies. Emphases on these two obligations vary among universities; some universities lean more to the former, others more towards the latter, but no university can wholly divest itself of either of these obligations. University teachers are similarly under these dual obligations. Teaching at an advanced level and fundamental research are the most important of the activities through which universities meet both these obligations.

The Obligations of University Teachers to their Society through Teaching: University teachers meet a paramount obligation in society through giving to their students the substantive knowledge and the methods of acquiring and assessing knowledge which will be valuable to them in their life after leaving university, in their occupational activities and outside them. They do this by teaching the students, up to the students' and their own utmost capacities, the most advanced knowledge in whatever the discipline in which their students are inscribed and do so in a manner appropriate to the student's level in his particular course of study. Teaching the students includes transmitting substantive knowledge to them and giving them an understanding of how such knowledge has been acquired or established. It involves teaching the student how to observe and reason about the phenomena with which his discipline deals. In giving him substantive knowledge and methods of thinking, it inducts the student or carries him further into some of the best elements of the intellectual and moral tradition of his civilisation—and to some extent of other civilisations—and it enables him thereby to appreciate the dignity and the value of knowledge in human life. Students who have been successfully taught the substance, principles and methods of a subject are simply by virtue of what they have gained from their teaching improved in their quality as human beings and hence as members of their society. What they should carry from this education into their life in society is a rational attitude, a respect for knowledge as a constituent of human action and as a constituent of the proper existence of a human being.

The teaching offered in a university also trains individuals for the practice of professions which require systematically studied knowledge for their practice and which are necessary for the well-being of society as a whole. Such professions include law, medicine, engineering, architecture and the administration of private and public enterprises. At the same time, it should be emphasized that the university is not the same as a vocational school or a polytechnic college. Purely technical knowledge which rests primarily on practical experience and not on an understanding of theoretical or fundamental principles does not have a central place in the teaching programmes of universities. The learning of manipulative skills is important for society. It is proper to have institutions for that purpose when "on the job training" is not enough. But that kind of training is not a task of the university. The tasks of the university are defined by the presence and necessity of advanced systematic, methodical and fundamental knowledge. It is not the distinction between useful and unuseful knowledge which draws the line between forms of training appropriate to universities and forms of training which are not their province. Rather it is the distinction between, on the one hand, training requiring, primarily, manual dexterity in the performance of complicated operations and in which practical experience is the basis of learning, and on the other, knowledge which is centred around certain fundamental principles and procedures, the mastery of which is required both for the practice of the professions and for the advancement of knowledge. It is the latter kind of knowledge which must be taught in universities. Clearly there are marginal cases; there can be disputes about the precise boundaries. But in principle the distinction is reasonably clear. Universities which do teach this kind of fundamental knowledge necessary for the advancement of knowledge and the practice of the professions are conferring invaluable benefits on their societies. This in fact is exactly what many universities are already doing. This does not preclude the teaching of particular courses for mature and experienced persons, already engaged in their respective professions; it only means that such courses must have a scientific or intellectual content.

The idea of being useful to society is being badly misinterpreted at present. Some reformers think that being useful to society means that universities should give up their concern with fundamental knowledge and with the rationale of evidence, experience and tradition and should concentrate on the training of young and middle-aged persons for the performance of the specific skilled operations which their society is willing to employ and pay for. These are, of course, perfectly legitimate educational activities, but not all of them must be taught in universities and they are certainly not all that universities should teach. Burdening universities with tasks which should be performed by other institutions, hampers the universities in their performance of those tasks which are necessary for society and which the universities alone can perform. It has the consequence too that the young are trained only for occupations which exist here and now. In a rapidly changing society, such an education can easily produce future unemployables, quite incapable of adjusting to new techniques.

The enlightenment of the wider public through "extension" courses presented away from the campus or of lectures open to the public but delivered on the campus is a very desirable activity but it does not fall directly within the circle of the primary obligation of university teachers. The main achievement of the university in the furtherance of public enlightenment should be sought through the education of the university's students in the substance and methods of thought of the various academic disciplines and through arousing and maintaining in them intellectual curiosity and sensibility which will persist in their life long after they have completed their studies and which they will diffuse through its presence in their professional activities.

The Obligations of University Teachers to their Society through Research: The only research which a university teacher should do is that in which he has an intellectual interest, since otherwise it is scarcely likely to be brought to a significant conclusion. He must consider whether his research will produce something of intellectual importance because it raises questions about a hitherto accepted theory, or supports a hitherto unsupported theory, or because it opens a way to a new theory. This motivation and expectation are, however, quite compatible with the intention that the results of the research should have practical value. This is indeed the case of much medical and agricultural research and much research in physics and chemistry. Intellectual significance and practical value are often intertwined in research.

There is one vital criterion to decide what kinds of research university teachers should undertake: this criterion is the probability that the research will contribute to fundamental knowledge. Although the conception of "fundamental" is not easy to formulate in a clear and comprehensive manner, some kinds of propositions are clearly of fundamental importance and others are clearly trivial and there is a large middle ground in which a judgement is more difficult to strike. Nevertheless, the idea provides a standard of assessment. It is a standard which each academic should apply when making a decision about what problems he will investigate. University teachers, except in cases of national emergency, should not undertake to do research of which they are not convinced that it might be a contribution to fundamental knowledge. The solution of strictly technical problems, which are of no scientific interest, for industry or government is not a part of the obligations of university teachers to their societies. If there were no other kinds of research institutions in society, there would be a justification for universities to undertake such research.

The criterion of the practical value of the results of the application of a piece of research is a supplementary one for academics. This does not mean that it need be secondary in the view of those bodies which support the research; for many of these it must be primary. Academics who seek to obtain funds from these bodies to enable them to do research which is scientifically interesting to them, often incline towards the scientifically interesting research which is likely to have useful practical consequences; this enhances the likelihood of obtaining the financial support they seek. Sometimes indeed the prospective practical value might be so great as to outweigh the smaller scientific value of the research in the eyes of the patrons as well as the scientists. Like the boundary between fundamental and trivial research, that between research which will have practical as well as basic scientific value and research which will have only practical value is by no means entirely clear. Nevertheless, there is a real difference between these two kinds of research and it is incumbent on the academic scientists to choose the former whenever they can.

The investigations with strictly practical intentions and consequences can certainly be of great value but universities are not the places where their execution will be to the most general advantage. For one thing, universities do not always have the equipment or the resources or the practical experience to do them with the greatest effectiveness and universities have other things to do which are not less urgent and from which they can be diverted by preoccupation with primarily practical problems. There are bound to be differences among the faculties and scholars of a university with respect to their conduct of research with a practical technological intention.

The professional schools of medicine, engineering, law and architecture will naturally do a great deal more research with immediate and indirect practical intentions than will some of the social and natural sciences and the humanities. But even in fields like mathematics and economics a good deal of the research will be intended to have practical applications. In all these fields, faculties and schools, however, the advancement of fundamental knowledge must be a concurrent intention. There is a wide variety of research institutions apart from universities in every modern society, and many of these exist for exactly the purpose of solving technological problems on the basis of existing fundamental and technological knowledge. There is a rough and reasonable division of labour between universities and these other research institutions and academic scientists should bear this in mind in making their choices.

It is by making contributions to fundamental knowledge, *i.e.*, to a deeper understanding of nature, man and his works and society that universities meet their primary obligations to society through research. The production of fundamental knowledge serves both the practical and the intellectual values of society. Society is not only a set of arrangements for solving practical problems; it is also the occasion for and in certain respects an expression of an aspiration to a deeper understanding. It is one of the many humane tasks of the universities to serve this latter aspiration which is common to most of the societies of Western civilisation.

A university which performs well the two basic tasks of teaching and research is going very far towards meeting its obligations to its society. It is producing educated, intellectually disciplined and equipped young persons capable of carrying on some of the most central practical and intellectual tasks of their society and it is expanding the society's stock of knowledge and deepening its understanding. These are, to say the least, services of the highest value.

The proper audience of the results of research should not be conceived only as other scientists as specialised as the producers of those results or as the "users" of such results in industry, government and other practically oriented organisations. The wider public should also be included in the audience. This public cannot be addressed in the same manner as scientifically qualified colleagues and "users" because it lacks the special training which would enable it to follow with full understanding the detailed technical accounts which appear in scientific and scholarly journals; nor do members of this wider public have the time needed to read all the papers and monographs in which these results are reported. There is therefore a necessity for the class of literature which may be called "popular science"; this "popular science" summarises in generally intelligible form the results of a large body of research and it does so in relatively short compass such as an intelligent and generally educated layman can find the time to read with understanding.

There are many reasons why academic scientists should contribute to "popular science". In the first place, inasmuch as scientific and scholarly research is intended to enhance the understanding of the universe and of man and his works, that understanding should be shared, in the appropriate form, by the largest possible section of the population in each society. There is also a perhaps less immediately lofty reason for making the intellectual results of scientific and scholarly research intelligible to the laity; the willingness of the laity to support scientific and scholarly research through the taxes it pays and through private philanthropic patronage depends to some degree on its appreciation of the intellectual and practical achievements of research. The widest possible diffusion of scientific knowledge is necessary too for the creation or maintenance of the "scientific ambience", *i.e.* the general lay appreciation of the legitimacy and necessity of science. It is in such an ambience that children and adolescents become interested in scientific work so that some of them decide to devote themselves to it. Without this steady flow of boys and girls interested in science and scholarship, the growth of these kinds of knowledge would be hampered. Although university teachers are not to be expected to add teaching in primary and secondary schools to their obligation, the writing of text books for these purposes alone or in collaboration with experienced school teachers is a proper and desirable activity for those academics who can do it.

All of these grounds for the wider diffusion of scientific and scholarly research beyond the audience of specialised scientists and scholars, "users" and university students place an additional obligation on academics. The obligation is a less continuous one than teaching and research and it does not apply in the same way to all academic scientists and scholars in the way in which the obligations of teaching and research do. Nevertheless the writing of text books and popular surveys of the state of knowledge over a broad range, is an obligation of the academic profession as a whole. It is something which the academic community as a whole owes to the wider public but only a small minority of its members can write such works. Because of this, such works may be written in collaboration with experienced text book writers or "scientific journalists", who know enough about a field to be able to understand technical expositions and who can express their understanding in a way intelligible to the laity, both adult and youthful.

The Obligation of Academic Scientists in the Practical Application of the Results of Research: Academic scientists do much research which has the practical application of its results as an ulterior or immediate objective. To do research which is intended to have practical consequences assumes that those consequences can be foreseen and rationally striven for. In fact, however, this assumption is not always valid. Scientists often discover things which they did not foresee; in the same way, there are practical consequences which cannot be foreseen. To what extent therefore should academic scientists do research the practical consequences of which they cannot foresee? It would be an extraordinary, unnecessary and illegitimate restriction on the freedom of scientific enquiry if scientists were required to predict with accuracy the practical consequences of their discoveries.

Nevertheless, in so far as practical consequences are, at least plausibly, foreseeable, and in so far as they disapprove of those foreseen practical consequences, academic scientists should be free to refuse to engage in the research which is thought to be necessary for the achievement of such consequences. As academic scientists, they are under an obligation to do research which will have intellectually significant or scientifically fundamental results. If they are as convinced as one can rationally be that the practical application of those results will be morally pernicious, without any compensating moral advantages, they should refuse to do that kind of research. They should abstain from performing experiments on human beings which have only slight scientific value and which will be foreseeably injurious to the particular persons on whom the experiments are performed or which can only result in injury to other persons.

The matter is, however, not as simple as it seems; unambiguous decisions are not easy to make. How can the possible benefits to many human beings be measured against the possible damage to the experimental subjects or animals? All that is possible is a very rough estimate of what is believed to be foreseeable; there can be no absolute guarantee that damaging consequences will not occur. It must be recognised that there are various degrees of risk in the assessment of possible damage and that there can be no unquestionable certainty in the prediction of outcomes.

It follows therefore that it is not reasonable to expect academic scientists to be held morally responsible for all the practical consequences of the application of the results of their research. It must be borne in mind that academic scientists who work on problems the solution of which is anticipated to be of practical importance are seldom the persons who undertake the application of those results; as long as the academic ethic of open publication is adhered to, the academic scientist is not in a position to prevent anyone who reads his account of his results from applying them if he can and wishes to do so. The only obligation laid on the academic scientist is to forbear from doing research which he is reasonably confident will have injurious effects on the persons involved in the research as members of the staff or as the subjects of experimentation. He is likewise under the obligation to forbear from performing research the results of which can clearly be applied only in a way injurious to the persons on whom they are applied and if these injurious effects are not substantially outweighed by the larger benefits of the application which are reasonably in prospect.

It will be seen that the obligation of openness of the communication of the results of research, an obligation which is central to the academic ethic, is incompatible with a demand that the academic scientist take on himself the responsibility for the application of the results of his research.

To assert that academic scientists are under an obligation to control the practical use of the results of their discoveries would require that they control access to those results. This amounts to the establishment of secrecy of the results of research already done or abstention from the investigation of certain subject-matters or problems about which knowledge might be injuriously applied. Such secrecy and abstention are repugnant to the academic ethic. The freedom of enquiry is not simply a negative freedom from the constraints of church, state and other earthly powers; it is a positive freedom to investigate whatever is adjudged to be intellectually significant.

One of the by-products of the intensified relationships of universities and governments and of universities and private business enterprises, arising from the capacity of university teachers to do research of practical value, has been the requirement of secrecy in connection with certain kinds of research. This is a new phenomenon in the history of universities. It is contrary to the tradition of science and scholarship to keep secret the results of research once the scientist or scholar has decided that his knowledge is reliable enough to lay before his colleagues. This problem does not arise for research done in governmental and industrial research institutions but it does appear in connection with research done in universities under contracts with governments and private firms.

(This assumes that these results meet prevailing intellectual standards. Editors of scientific journals might refuse to publish these results but they are justified in doing so only if they and their advisers regard them as too trivial or as insufficiently sound scientifically but this is another matter.)

What should be the relationship of academic scientists with research workers employed under those restrictive conditions? There can be no question about the access of these latter scientists to the published results of academic scientists; these are in the public arena and are available to anyone who wishes to see them. To what extent should an academic scientist make his still unpublished results available to scientists of these "secretive" institutions? There is no significant difference between transmitting still unpublished results and the publication of the same results which will shortly become available to anyone who wishes to and can read them. But what about situations in which scientists in universities, deliberately and by agreement with the authorities of the university, withhold their results from publication (or do not distribute preprints) for a stipulated period during which their application is considered by private business enterprise?

In practice, there is nothing amiss if academic scientists communicate their unpublished results to scientists in these secret zones just as they would to scientists in other universities as long as they make clear that they will and actually do publish their results in publicly available scientific journals when they think they are ready and if they are confident that their results will not be plagiarised or used for purposes which might be harmful to the laity. If the period of withholding is only about a few weeks or months, there is in fact little or no infringement on the obligation of open publication because the period between the date of submission to a journal and the date of publication is frequently much longer.

The practice of the openness of scientific and scholarly knowledge, except under conditions of extreme emergency, is one of the chief obligations of academic scientists and scholars. The principle of the autonomy of the university requires that decisions about what should be studied, how it should be studied and whether the results should be published should be in the hands of academics and not in the hands of non-academic persons in political organisations, churches, business firms, governments and armies. It is because academics are best able to assess and decide about academic things that they may legitimately lay claim to the autonomy of universities. This autonomy is infringed when external institutions decide what research should be carried on in universities and assure themselves of this right to determine the choice of research problems in universities through provision in a contract made when the grant of financial support is given.

The matter is very complicated. Ever since academic scientific research began to exceed in cost what could be borne by the ordinary university budget, the carrying out of research projects conceived by academics in the natural sciences, and increasingly in the social sciences, has depended on the availability of external financial resources. If a patron, governmental, philanthropic or industrial, did not wish to support a particular piece of research and if no alternative means could be found to provide the needed financial resources, the particular research could not be done. Since the middle of the nineteenth century, industrialists have approached individual scientists—as certain German chemicals manufacturers once approached Justus Liebig—with the request that they investigate certain topics of interest to those industrialists in return for which they would support the research, including provision for a certain number of graduate students, etc. This was a step towards the determination of the choice of research-subjects by an external power. Arrangements such as have recently been established at the Massachusetts Institute of Technology might turn out to be an institutional establishment of such external determination of the choice of topics for research. Such an arrangement would probably also bring with it the restriction on the freedom to publish the results of research until they have been patented by the extra-academic patron. The arrangement about patents however continues an already existing practice in the patenting of processes, substances and mechanisms discovered or invented in universities. Universities have been in the custom of patenting discoveries or inventions of members of their academic staffs. This has sometimes involved a short delay in the publication of the results of the particular research until the patent has been granted. There is nothing in this procedure contrary to the academic ethic, as long as the results of the research are published and thus made accessible to other scientists.

Recent developments also raise other questions. Certain discoveries and techniques of research in university laboratories—recombinant DNA is the most prominent—have in recent years turned out to have potentialities for ever greater commercial profitability. Numerous industrial enterprises are being envisaged for the development and production of substances discovered in this field by academic scientists. Should the individual academic scientist make his discoveries available to a particular firm and to no other in return for munificent support of his research and large honoraria? Should he establish a firm of his own through which he can exploit his discovery and which he will operate as an ordinary business enterprise? Should he simply publish his results in the established scientific journals, as scientists have always done ever since scientific journals came into existence, and allow his university to obtain a patent which will bring income to it? Should the university itself form an industrial corporation to develop and sell the knowledge of the processes, substances or mechanisms discovered or invented in its laboratories and patented by it? Should the university take out the patent in its own name and then license it to industrial enterprises which wish to produce the substance or to use the process or mechanism for their own commercial profit? This is an unprecedented situation in the history of universities; it is difficult at present to promulgate the obligations of universities because the patterns and ramifications of the relationship of academic scientists and private business enterprises are still unclear. Certain things are indisputable: academic scientists, while holding full-time academic appointments, should not become the owners and managers of business enterprises which will take up most of their time and energy. Academic scientists furthermore should not be governed in their choice of research-problems by the prospect of becoming rich from the commercial application of their discoveries. Recently there have been cases of university teachers who had created survey, statistical information and economic advisory services. The founder and owner of one of these recently sold his institute for $10,000,000.00. Is there anything contrary to the academic ethic in such entrepreneurial activities?

In principle, this question is much like the question of the propriety of university teachers entering external non-academic employment while holding full-time appointments at universities. There are precedents which would appear to justify the conduct of a private business enterprise by an academic who has a contract with his university for full-time teaching and research. Some professors of medicine have very lucrative private practices "on the side"; professors of law, accounting and engineering and architecture have private practices or act in a private capacity in special cases and many serve as consultants and receive substantial incomes from these activities, in addition to their regular salaries from the university. There is a good argument for such activities to the extent that they infuse the knowledge gained by university teachers through such activities into their teaching and research. It might however also be a distraction from the primary responsibility of teaching and research.

External business activities are subject to criticism if the academics involved skimp on their service to the university in teaching and research in order to carry on with their "private practice". If it can be done without skimping, then it might be beneficial to the teaching, if not of the research, conducted at the university because it will enable the teacher to give the students knowledge of the most recent development in the practical activity for which the students are preparing themselves.

Association with commercial or industrial enterprises presents additional possibilities of diverting a university teacher from his obligations. The requirements of time and energy are not the only things which a university teacher owes to teaching, research and other duties within the university; there might also be a conflict between the pecuniary interest of the firm with which the university teacher is associated and the pecuniary interest of his university. If, for example, an academic is the owner or a member of the board of directors of a firm manufacturing scientific instruments which seeks to sell its products to the department of which its owner or director is a member, the latter is obviously involved in a conflict of interest. It is necessary that such conflicts of interests be avoided by the university teacher.

The issue here is the extent to which the external activity hinders the performance of the primary obligations of the university teacher for teaching and research. If the business enterprises conducted by university teachers do not require their active and continuous management and require no more than about one day weekly and if they do not bring their owners into conflicts of interests or the exploitation of the resources placed at their disposal by the university for their own private profit, such activities are compatible with the academic obligations of university teachers.

The issues of whether academics may supplement their university salaries by income gained through consultation or the conduct of business enterprise or by any other means and whether such external earnings are to be reported to the administration of the university are to be resolved in accordance with the primary obligation of any academic who holds an appointment for full-time service in teaching, research and other university duties. As long as a university teacher does not fail in his primary academic obligations, his income, assuming that it is legally gained, is entirely his own affair.

The Obligations of University Teachers to their Societies through the Performance of Services: There are also more specific ways which university teachers are sometimes called upon or urged to serve their society. These services are of many kinds. One of the most common of these services in the English-speaking world used to be the conduct of extension courses for adults who were not regular students of the university; another has been the writing of articles in popular periodicals and newspapers and books for general circulation in which they set forth in relatively easily intelligible form the results of their research and their reflections. To these have been added in more recent years broadcasting on radio and television. Other services are the performance of special kinds of social welfare services, such as the provision of medical care and legal services for the poor, the conduct of mental health centres, the management of day-nurseries for small children or the organisation of educational and recreational activities for secondary schoolchildren of the neighbourhood of the university; in some universities, departments of education have conducted primary and secondary schools. Others have entailed the performance of research including very descriptive kinds of quantitative social research or elementary soil analysis for farmers or the testing of materials for local industrial enterprises or municipal governments. Some universities have developed industrial research bureaus and survey research institutes, which, on a contractual basis, conduct surveys for governmental and private organisations. Still other services which universities sometimes have performed for non-academic bodies are special training courses, *e.g.* for colonial administrators, Negro business enterprisers or for policemen or civil servants of the middle or lower ranks, or for employees of private business firms desiring to be brought up to date in the knowledge which they need for their work. There are also services in management, for example, offered by universities against payment. (Athletic events and games are presented to the general public by many American state universities and other American higher educational institutions in anticipation of substantial income from television-broadcasting firms in return for the privilege of presenting these very popular spectacles.)

Every one of these services has some justification. Some of them bring income to the university which is especially welcome when it is harder to obtain funds from other sources. Some are useful to the local community in which the university is located. Others are part of the "public relations" of the university which have the justification of causing tax-payers and the public at large to look with favour on the university. Some of these services are intellectual and are continuous in content with the activities which are central in the life of universities. Extension courses, special courses of lectures open to the wider public, popular accounts of specific projects and whole fields of research are made available to a wider public; some of the extension services sometimes also enable graduate students to acquire experience in teaching. The special training courses are built around the specialised knowledge of some of the teachers of the university, although sometimes more or less qualified persons are appointed specifically for the teaching of those courses. Some of the other services such as the provision of staff for legal aid clinics are also akin to the central activities of the universities in so far as they give students the opportunity to learn how to apply the knowledge they have been acquiring in their studies. Still other services have little to do with the intellectual tasks of universities but might be desirable as humanitarian undertakings or as a means of assuaging the animosity of "town" against "gown" or of maintaining the immediate social environment of the university and making life more attractive for students and teachers.

All of these services are however only of marginal significance in so far as they do not contribute to the main task of teaching and discovery. If research done on contract with industrial firms or government is also the kind of research which furthers the advancement of fundamental knowledge as well as serving the practical aims of firms or government, then it is acceptable for a member of the academic staff of the university to undertake it—assuming, of course, that he has an intellectual interest in it, that it does not distract him from more important research and teaching in which he was already engaged and if the results can be published and shared with students and colleagues. If the training courses for police or civil servants or employees of business firms involves teaching at a level appropriate to a university and if they present fundamental social science knowledge in an applied form, that too is a service which it is acceptable for a university teacher to undertake. If it is less than that, then it should not be undertaken by university teachers, and their universities should not ask them to do so.

The line which divides services which have an advanced scientific or scholarly content in teaching or research from those which are no more than services which some other institution like a police training-college or a civil service staff-college or a municipal governmental statistical bureau or the census bureau of the central government performs as part of its routine activities, is not a very precisely definable line. Nevertheless, university teachers and those who represent them should ask themselves whether when they provide these services they are not stepping over that line. If they are over that line, they should not be undertaken.

The Obligations of University Teachers to their Societies through Political and Publicistic Activities: It is in the nature of intellectual activities to make critical assessments of any received tradition. There would be no advancement of knowledge in any field by university teachers if they accepted unquestioningly the traditions of knowledge which are presented to them. The very advancement of knowledge rests on the discernment of gaps and insufficiencies in the tradition. The reception of and respect for the tradition of one's subject coupled simultaneously with a critical attitude towards those parts of it with which they are actively engaged are an obligation of the academic calling. This complex relationship to the tradition of knowledge is an essential feature of teaching as well as research in universities. Good teaching includes teaching how to be rationally critical towards what is taught and learned from the tradition.

This critical attitude has not been confined to the particular fields of specialised study and research. It has extended beyond the boundaries of any special field. This has been especially characteristic of university teachers—and students—in the nineteenth and twentieth centuries. It is in fact inseparable from the great achievements of universities. In some countries, it was the churches or rather traditional religious beliefs which first came under the critical study and evaluation of academic scholars. Since the latter part of the preceding century and through most of the present one, the critical attitudes of university teachers, especially in the social sciences, have been extended towards existing political, social and economic arrangements in their societies.

One concomitant of this critical attitude has been the increased political interest and activity of academics. University teachers in the years since the Second World War have been drawn into political controversies and movements to a greater degree than ever before. University teachers have now become forces in the public and political life of their respective societies. The exercise of this critical disposition—unequally distributed among different disciplines—brings with it obligations.

University teachers are members of their larger society with the rights and obligations of all citizens. They also have additional obligations. These arise from their possession of special bodies of knowledge and their expertise on subjects which are very pertinent to problems of great importance to the wider public and its organisations and to government. The activity of university teachers, outside research and university citizenship, is addressed to laymen, *i.e.*, persons who have less knowledge than they themselves possess. Just as in their capacity as teachers, they deal with students who know less than they do, as citizens engaging in a variety of political and publicistic activities, they are constantly in contact with other persons who do not have as much knowledge as the academics themselves about the particular subjects of which they possess complex knowledge. (In their domestic, convivial and communal relationships, their large stock of complex knowledge has no bearing, although they are at times accorded a large measure of deference in recognition of this stock of knowledge regardless of its irrelevance to the situation in question.)

Academics have all sorts of interests and aspirations—just as do physicians and lawyers and engineers and factory workers. They are interested in higher salaries and security of tenure. They are often politically partisan. Neither their private desires nor their wishes for certain economic and social policies to be carried out nor their preference for particular economic, social and political arrangements, permit them to suspend the obligation of telling the truth about any particular subject as it has been arrived at by careful and critical study of the relevant evidence; this is the obligation which they have taken upon themselves by entry into the academic profession. This obligation is still valid, even though many infringe upon it. What should be thought of a physician who is careless in his diagnosis and treatment of a poor person, or of a person whose religion is different from his own; what should be thought of an engineer who neglects the principles of the strength of materials when designing a building for a person of whose political or religious views he disapproves? Or of a lawyer who having accepted a client, does not do his best to win the case because he disagrees with the client's political or religious views or disapproves of the client's moral qualities or temperament? As with physicians, lawyers, and engineers, so it is with the university teacher: he must not allow his political partisanship or any other predilections to influence his teaching or the collection and analysis of data in research. Admittedly it is more difficult for a teacher to control this tendency in the social sciences or some branches of the humanities than in the natural sciences but that only makes it more of an obligation to watch and discipline himself.

In his research, in addition to the control imposed by his own moral self-scrutiny and self-discipline, the academic is watched over by his colleagues. If he infringes on the obligations of painstakingness in observation, or of rigour in analysis, the editors of the journals to which he submits his papers and the referees selected by the editors and the reviewers of his monographs are likely to catch him out; even if he gets through their critical assessment, some of the scientists or scholars who read his published work are very likely to detect his factual mistakes and his misinterpretations and his work will be refuted or neglected. His reputation in his scientific or scholarly community will be damaged. External control within the community of his fellow-scientists or fellow-scholars reinforces the self-discipline which he learned as a student to exercise. These are all situations in which he is being observed and assessed by his peers. An equally demanding situation does not exist where his audience knows less about his subject than he does.

As a custodian of the best knowledge available through the best procedures of discovery and interpretation, respect for the truth is the unrenounceable obligation of the university teacher in all the public activities in which he engages. The difficulties lie in knowing just what is the truth about the particular subject-matter under consideration; this very uncertainty about the validity of a particular proposition requires that it should not be asserted in a dogmatic way, as if it were unquestionable.

The obligation of an academic as a teacher to avoid as well as he can the assertion of his own political and ethical views in the guise of scientific or scholarly knowledge obtains also in his relations with individuals or institutions whom he serves as an expert adviser or consultant. Scrupulousness in adherence to the strictest standards of truthfulness are incumbent on him in all these situations. This entails, on the one hand, the avoidance of distortions impelled by political and moral ideals or partisanship on behalf of particular political movements and, on the other, a willingness to admit ignorance and insufficient knowledge. Even under the favourable conditions of presenting carefully prepared material in a class-room, this is a difficult requirement to meet. It is more difficult for an academic who engages in public debates, oral or written, in public meetings or on television or radio or in short articles or interviews in newspapers and periodicals.

Is an academic bound, in his publicistic and political activities and in activities as a consultant, by his academic obligations to adhere to the standards of intellectual integrity which he observes in his teaching and research? Does the fact that he is a university teacher impose any restraint on his freedom in the public sphere to which laymen are not equally subject? It does, in so far as his representations purport to be based on careful study and as long as they claim the authority of expertise gained through scientific and scholarly research. It certainly does, in so far as, in his public action, he allows himself to be identified by his academic connection and rank; in such cases, he is allowing himself to claim, or to have claimed on his behalf, the authority which is acknowledged to inhere in methodically acquired expert knowledge, disinterestedness and abstention from passionate partisanship. But even if he does not allow the name of his university to appear alongside his own name—in so far as he has any control over that—he is still under the obligation of intellectual scrupulousness which he accepted when he became a university teacher. He has also the obligation not to betray the trust which is given him when laymen look to him for objective knowledge and responsible judgement.

Academics who speak in public about the issues which engage public opinion almost always allow the presumption that they speak with the authority of scientific and scholarly study. Even where their sponsors have invited them on the assumption that the analyses and arguments of the academic person will support their own partisan position, they do so also on the assumption that the academic in question will enjoy special attention and respect because he will be presumed by the audience to speak with the authority conferred by intensive and scrupulous study of the issues involved. This gives special force to the duty of the university teacher to respect the obligations which are entailed in the custodianship and representation of scientific and scholarly knowledge. Even if they were to disregard the expectations of their audience, the obligation to speak the truth would still exist. Legally, an academic is entitled to tell as many half-truths and falsehoods in public as any lay politician, journalist or agitator. He is legally entitled to be as demagogic and misleading as any other unscrupulous citizen. It might be claimed that a citizen should not be handicapped in his political conduct by his membership in the academic profession, that the political sphere is different from the academic sphere and that the obligations of the latter are not valid in the former. Such a claim would be wrong.

This claim to exemption of the academic from special obligations in the public sphere might be more acceptable if the two spheres were entirely disjoined from each other. They are, however, not so disjoined because knowledge of the kind which the academic represents as a teacher and scientist also enters or can enter into action in the political sphere and that is the reason why he is invited to speak and is listened to. Furthermore, the academic in the sphere of public discussion seldom divests himself of the appurtenances of his academic life, he uses his academic title or titles, and he allows his academic connections to be known; in doing so, he allows it to be believed that his detachment and his objectivity of judgement as a scientist or scholar are brought into play when he participates in controversy about political matters. In fact, he would not have such easy access to the public forum if he did not have these academic qualifications and if it were not believed that his assertions carried with them the authority of long and scrupulous study. The hearing which an academic receives from laymen, whether they be legislators, civil servants or ordinary citizens, is more attentive and more deferential because of the laymen's belief that academics have a special qualification to speak truthfully about the issue at hand, because they have a detached cast of mind as well as a large stock of relevant and reliable knowledge on the subject at issue. For these reasons, an academic transmitting or intimating knowledge in the public and political sphere has the same obligations as are entailed in the quest for and the transmission of knowledge in the academic sphere.

Academics often do not have the same sense of obligation to their fellow-citizens as they have to their pupils who come to them presumably to learn what the academics have acquired by their studies. The position of the pupil is also different from that of a political antagonist or of a potential supporter. The student has come presumably to have his mind furnished and guided and many teachers take seriously the responsibility arising from the fact that the student has entrusted himself to his teachers. Even though a lay audience might accord trust to an academic, that very fact, however, is sometimes regarded by academics as an advantage to be exploited rather than as imposing an obligation. The rules of the game are generally regarded as less exacting in the public sphere; there is more acceptance of a knockabout atmosphere, more of a tradition of the permissibility of overstatement and suppression. This is one of the reasons why academics when they are politically engaged, regard themselves as absolved from the exigent obligations which many of them feel compelled to honour in their academic activities.

On the contrary, rather than being absolved, the academic in political and publicistic activity has a special obligation which is incumbent on him in consequence of his possession of an elaborate body of scientific or scholarly knowledge and more generally because the public standing which he is usually glad to accept is granted him by virtue of his presumed commitment to such knowledge. He can, it is true, be criticised for what he says in the public sphere but there are bound to be many persons in his audience who are not in a position to render an intellectually qualified criticism of his assertions and who are nonetheless citizens with the obligation to make up their minds about the general line of policy which public bodies should follow. These persons are entitled, when they open their minds or at least give their attention to an academic speaking in public, to have as truthful an account of the events about which they have to pass judgement as long and diligent study makes possible. The academics who participate in public political discussion have an obligation to these persons, not really different from that which they have to their students. In both cases, they are addressing themselves to persons who presumably know less about the subject under consideration than they themselves do. Academics who address themselves in speech or in writing to a larger public in the field of their expertise or in a field in which they are presumed to have expertise should regard themselves as bound by the trust which their audience grants them as scholars or scientists. But even if the audience has no special expectations, the academics themselves still have the obligations which they accepted when entering the academic career. Logically there is nothing in any proposition which requires that the person who knows it should avoid distorting it or suppressing it. Nonetheless, the ethical postulates of the high appreciation of the truths attained through systematic research and analysis and of the value of striving for them, which are entailed in the entry into and practice of an academic career, are incompatible with a cavalier attitude towards such truths and towards the evidence they require.

It has been said that the obligations of the academic acting in the public sphere are greater when he speaks with the authority of an expert in his own field of professional study than they are when he speaks outside his field of expertise. This is doubtful, regardless of whether he is speaking in his field of expertise or speaking outside it. He still receives attention because of his standing as an academic, as a member of a university, bearing the titles and degrees which are granted him for achievement as a scientist or scholar, and this attention carries with it these inescapable obligations. The moral limitations on the freedom of expression in the public sphere are therefore by no means entirely confined to social scientists and humanistic scholars; infringements on these limitations are, in fact, often committed by natural scientists too.

Many biochemists, physicists and astronomers are certainly not experts on the matters on which they occasionally hold forth in the political arena. They are deferred to because it is thought that they are practising the same detachment and disinterestedness in their judgements about public matters that they evince in dealing with scientific problems. This deference should not be exploited although it often is exploited. If, as is frequently the case, their qualifications in substantive knowledge for receiving the attention of the public are not superior to those of any other citizen, they should not seek to enhance the persuasiveness of their arguments and analyses by alleging that the latter have been arrived at by strictly scientific methods and by allowing their academic connections and status to be adduced to fortify their authority.

For about eight decades, and to a much greater degree in recent years, academics have been conducting political activities through "open letters" in which the signatories list their universities, rank, and sometimes departments. This is an exploitation of public confidence in the integrity of scientists and scholars, but it is a very minor aspect of the problem. Even if this particular kind of exploitation were to cease and if academics were to throw themselves into politics as professional politicians do, they would still have the obligations arising from their professional acceptance of the custodianship of knowledge, not just of specific and factual knowledge in particular disciplines, but of the general rules of its acquisition and communication.

When one has entered voluntarily into the academic profession, one commits oneself to observance of the norms of disinterested scrutiny of evidence and of logical reasoning. It is an obligation to which one submits as a condition of entering the profession. Of course, this is not done in the form of an oath but that does not make the obligation less binding. This obligation extends to every sphere in which the academic acts in a capacity in which academic knowledge is involved and in which the academic intimates or asserts explicitly that his opinions carry the authority of disciplined study.

These obligations of the university teacher in political and publicistic activities are largely restrictive. They do not require that academics carry on political activities; they require only that when academics do so they should not play fast and loose with truths. There is however one object for which political activity is positively required by the academic ethic. It is an obligation of academic citizenship to look after the well-being of universities as intellectual institutions and not only the well-being of their own universities but of universities throughout their respective countries. Since universities are now so intimately dependent on governments, it is obligatory for academics to follow closely the activities of governments as they affect universities and to make representations to governments about existing and alternative policies. It goes without saying that the manner of these representations should conform with the stipulations of the academic ethic regarding other political and publicistic activities of university teachers. There is no obligation on academics to be supine or silent in the face of what they think to be wrong policies of governments, either about universities and scientific and scholarly research any more than there is for them to abstain from political and publicistic activities generally. But whereas there is no positive obligation on them as university teachers to engage actively in the latter, there is an obligation derived from the obligation of academic citizenship to concern themselves about the effects of governmental activities on academic things.

It is clear that all academics must engage equally in making representations for the protection and promotion of learning. It is undesirable that such representations should be left exclusively or primarily to the administrative officers of universities and to the professional officials of learned societies and academic associations.

The burden which is laid upon the academic of adhering to the required norms in his public and political activity is heavier than it is in the academic sphere proper; in the public and political spheres he bears it unaided by the disciplining and critical assessment of his academic colleagues. In the public and political spheres, he does not have the corrective protection which he receives in the academic sphere in the form of discriminating approval or disapproval of colleagues who are well qualified and who are the primary audience of scientific and scholarly works.

An academic in the public sphere does not have the same external constraints on him as he has when he is conducting research and presenting its results to his colleagues. In the public sphere, he is not subject to measured, painstaking assessment by persons who know as much as he does about the very things he is speaking or writing about. He does not even have the vaguely compelling discipline which sometimes comes from the physical presence or proximity of his colleagues. He may indeed be criticised for his statements by those academics who disagree with him, but, since the intellectual standard of public discourse is often regarded by academics as less exigent than that which should prevail within the academic community, their criticism of demagogic public statements by an academic colleague is often on the same level as the statements they criticise. Those who disagree with his political conclusions might censure them but more usually they will simply castigate him for being "radical" or "reactionary", according to their tastes.

In summary, it must be recognised that addressing an academic audience in a colloquium or at a scientific congress or in the pages of a journal or a monograph is different from addressing an audience of laymen, whether they are ordinary citizens at a public meeting or readers of a newspaper or a general magazine or whether they are legislators taking testimony before a legislative committee or civil servants reading a memorandum. In all the latter cases, the university teacher is not only addressing the laity, he is also having to make his scientific or scholarly knowledge intelligible to them. Because they are laymen, the knowledge given to them must be presented in an inevitably simplified form. It is true that in addressing undergraduates in a class-room at fairly elementary levels of the subject, allowances must be made which need not and generally are not made in addressing more advanced students. In simplifying for undergraduates, however, the teacher is aided by the tradition which is incorporated into text books; these embody an art of simplification for beginning students which has been developed over many years and this is a great aid to the teacher. Furthermore, the teacher is not expected to be omniscient about things which are still not known. Serious students do not expect a teacher to know things which no scientist or scholar has yet learned through research. The students know that they are attending an elementary course and they usually know that there is much that is still unknown to their teachers, even to the most distinguished ones.

A lay audience has different expectations. It listens to a scientist or a scholar because it believes that he is asserting definitive truths about the conditions or processes of which he is speaking. Such a lay audience appreciates less than an academic audience the imperfections of knowledge; it frequently assumes that a scientist or scholar "has the answers" to the problems under discussion. Furthermore, in his public activities, the academic is frequently constrained by the short time or small space which is allowed him; even before a legislative committee, he is not allowed the amplitude of a 30-hour lecture course, or of a seminar running over a whole term. In addition to this, his exposition is frequently oral in mode, subject to interruptions and to his own feeling of the need to make his points strikingly to the audience which is not well informed and which he will not see again once his brief exposition is finished.

The university teacher in writing for a newspaper or a general periodical is under similar constraints. The audience and often the editor are not as qualified as his students are in their classes and seminars, they expect him to deliver a definitive answer and they require that he do it briefly. In the face of all difficulties, the problems of simplification are exacerbated. The simplification of scientific knowledge is a very demanding task. Most scientists and scholars are not skilful in it. It is sometimes done very effectively in magazines like *Scientific American*, *The New Scientist* and *la Recherche* but it is done in these journals with the aid of very experienced and knowledgeable editors and with the expectation that a good part of the readership already has considerable scientific knowledge.

The inherent difficulties of simplification of scientific knowledge and the plain fact that on many of the issues under contention in the public and political spheres there is no definitively demonstrable knowledge are additional obstacles. These obstacles are quite distinct from the temptations of partisan contention, but they add to the difficulties of fulfilling the obligations of university teachers when they engage in political and publicistic activities. They do not, however, invalidate the obligations of the university teacher who engages in such activities.

The Obligations of University Teachers to Government: University teachers have been turned to increasingly by governments as consultants and advisers. They have been invited increasingly to serve as members of commissions to prepare reports for both the legislative and executive branches and to appear as experts before committees of legislative bodies. They are also sometimes brought as experts into judicial proceedings. Their counsel is sought because they are presumed to know more about certain matters and to have more detached and better schooled judgement on those matters than the appointed civil servants in the higher ranks or than the elected legislators and their staffs or than ordinary witnesses. Academic advisers are not sought out by politicians and civil servants or lawyers because of their superior knowledge of moral truths; they are not chosen as moral guides and counsellors but as experts who have studied and mastered certain subjects. They have been chosen because they can advise civil servants and others on the best, *i.e.*, the most efficacious means of achieving their particular objectives or because they can analyse more reliably the ramifications and possible repercussions of a proposed policy or because they know more about the facts under contention. In the course of giving advice about prospective policies, they often do not confine themselves to the means of attaining given objectives; they also help to redefine the objectives by analysing them more closely, by showing what their costs and benefits are likely to be. Sometimes they are explicitly invited to argue for a particular policy; sometimes they do so unavowedly in the course of making recommendations about the best means of attaining particular ends, with minimal costs with respect to other ends. They are also invited, especially by legislators, because of their known political sympathies and the prestige which their testimony will confer on the objectives the legislators wish to promote.

Academics are seldom invited to serve as consultants or advisers because of their "wisdom" in the delineation of the ultimate ends of policy. They are invited and given credence because they are thought to be in possession of more complex—and more reliable—knowledge of the subject in question than are the elected and appointed officials who are supposed to deal with those subjects. In some cases this might be so. But in many of those cases, the knowledge possessed by the academics in these subjects is too suppositious, too uncertain to provide an incontrovertible element in the discussion to which it purports to contribute exactly such an element. Often the research which has been done does not allow for a definitive and unambiguous answer to the questions which should be answered, if one alternative of policy is to be chosen over others. Even specially commissioned research seldom, if ever, produces indisputable answers to the questions which have been put to it.

What are the obligations of academic scientists and scholars in such circumstances? One obligation is not to abuse the trust which has been accorded to them on the presumption that they actually possess certain and definitive knowledge which can replace the ignorance and uncertainty of the laity. This implies the obligation to restrain themselves from overstating the degree of certainty of their knowledge and from contending for one alternative over others with a tone of conviction which the existing state of knowledge on the relevant subjects does not justify.

Since the politicians and civil servants know less about the relevant subjects than the scientists and scholars, however uncertain their knowledge is, should the latter be reluctant to press their own preferences? It could be said that, since after all, a decision must be made, and since the relevant facts have not been unambiguously established, the academic is as entitled as the legislator and civil servant or as any ordinary citizen to press his own preferences. This argument fails to recognise that the legislators were elected and the civil servants were appointed to make decisions under conditions of uncertainty and that ordinary citizens are not invited to do what scientific advisers and consultants are invited to do. The academic is called in, not in his capacity as an ordinary citizen for the purpose of making a decision under conditions of uncertainty, but rather because his knowledge puts him in a different position than that of an ordinary citizen and is thought to enable him to reduce or eliminate that uncertainty. If he cannot do that, it does not follow that he is entitled to attempt to usurp the powers and responsibilities assigned to elected and appointed officials.

A university teacher who is invited by a governmental or private body as an expert to advise about a matter in which a decision calls upon scientific knowledge is in a position not entirely unlike that of a teacher before his students or an academic addressing an audience which knows less about his subject than he does. A university teacher is under an exacting obligation to assess and disclose the reliability of the knowledge which he is transmitting to his students and to be as careful as possible to make sure that what he asserts as valid knowledge is not determined by his economic and political interests or desires. It is the same with respect to his activity in research. It is no different when he engages in public or political contention. It is no different when he serves as an adviser or consultant to government. It is not easy, especially in the social sciences, where methods of analysis are not so rigorous and where so many of the subjects studied are also the objects of political contention to separate one's valid knowledge from what one's political and moral ends incline one to believe. Yet the distinction is a valid one and academics who are consultants or advisers on the basis of their "expertise" should attempt to observe it with the same conscientiousness that they exercise in their research.

Before the Second World War, there were usually relatively few opportunities available to tempt academics into excessive diversion of their time and energy into external activities. In Western Europe and North America, university appointments have mainly been appointments on full-time and by and large university teachers have conformed with expectations that most of their time would be spent on academic activities, with a very flexible allowance being made for the performance of various services and public and publicistic activities. In Italy, it was not rare for academics to be members of parliament while retaining their academic posts and looking after them as best they could. (In the countries of Latin America where university teaching was not a full-time occupation, it was expected that they would conduct private professional practices or would have some other sources of income such as governmental employment or private business.) After the Second World War, both the opportunities and inclinations of university teachers to engage in extra-academic pursuits have increased markedly.

The service of government in consultative or advisory capacities, like political and publicistic activities, presents problems in the fulfilment of the primary obligations of university teachers. All of these activities outside the university are usually undertaken while the person in question continues to hold a full-time academic post; they all require time and energy. Apart from conventions or regulations regarding the numbers of lectures or courses he is expected to give in an academic session, it has been generally accepted that the university teacher should be free to decide for himself how he will allocate his time among his various concerns. It has usually been assumed that, apart from his classes and seminars, he will spend his time primarily in research and study for the preparation of courses, with smaller amounts of time to be used for examinations and other tasks of university administration. University teachers who spend a great deal of time in the delivery of lectures to lay audiences, or who become "television stars" or who write a great deal for newspapers and general periodicals have sometimes caused eyebrows to be raised. Some universities have placed limits on the magnitude of income from non-academic activities but it is not a widespread practice. Since there have been no precise stipulations as to how much time teachers should spend in such external activities, these cases of excessive participation in such activities have very seldom caused more than mild, informal disapproval.

As long as a university teacher holds an appointment on full-time at a university, the proportion of his time which he devotes to advice and consultation for government, like the proportion of his time which he devotes to consultation for private business firms or to the conduct of a private business firm or private professional practices of his own must be limited. A reasonable rule would stipulate that not more than one day each week be used for external activities regardless of whether they are for political activities or consultation as an "expert" for private business firms or for government or for the conduct of a private professional practice.

What has been said about the special obligations of academics in political and publicistic activities or as consultants or advisers to adhere to the same standards of probity in the presentation of their knowledge that they observe in their research and teaching does not apply with the same force to those academics who cease to be academics by accepting elective or appointive office in government. It is right that many universities require that any of their members who accept such offices take a leave-of-absence of specified duration. These non-academic activities must be carried on continuously and all the time and their practice is not compatible with the fulfilment of the obligations of an academic appointment.

It is, however, not only a matter of time. It is also a matter of the nature of the primary obligations and necessities of the life of a politician and civil servant. The scientific or scholarly validity of knowledge is not a primary concern of politicians and civil servants; they have moreover no obligation to add to the stock of fundamental knowledge by reliable methods nor have they any obligation to transmit the substance of that knowledge while training its recipients in the modes of acquiring and assessing knowledge. The practice of requiring that academics who become legislators or civil servants take leave-of-absence is necessitated not only by the incompatibility of the demands in time and energy of the two kinds of occupational activities. It is also a recognition that the obligations of the two are different from each other in substance. The recognition of the fundamental difference in the respective tasks of these two kinds of activity is an acknowledgement of the tension which is engendered when the academic engages in activities in the public sphere. As long as he is an academic and respects his obligations as an academic he cannot allow himself to act like any other non-academic participant in political and publicistic activities or like any businessman or private or public administrator. The academic cannot "let himself go"; he is constrained by the obligations imposed by commitment to the life of scientific and scholarly knowledge, the rules of methodical observation, rational analysis and critical assessment.

Note on Accountability to Government: In recent years, the issue of the accountability of scientists and scholars receiving grants from governments for research, has been raised. This is a much more limited and special issue but it merits some attention in a discussion of the obligations of university teachers to their government. It is perfectly reasonable that scientists and scholars should be accountable for how they spend the money which governments make available to them for their research. There is no doubt that there is an obligation of accountability. The only issue is the extent of their accountability. They are certainly under the obligation which is required by law to show that the funds were expended only on legitimate objects directly connected with the research for which they were granted. They are also under obligation to work conscientiously on these projects; this is part of their obligation to knowledge. They should not however be regarded as under obligation to specify the exact amount of time in hours and minutes they spend on the project; they should also not be placed under obligation to conduct the research in precisely the manner which they specified on the application, if in the course of it, a new idea occurs to them as to how to do the research better than first occurred to them when they applied for the funds. This is in accordance with the freedom of investigation which is a part of the academic freedom to teach and to do research according to their best lights. The academic is accountable to governments for honest dealing in doing his research but nothing is gained by government or by knowledge if an academic scientist is forced to submit reports in an unrealistic degree of detail.

The Obligations of University Teachers to their Societies Generally: Does a university teacher owe loyalty to the constitution and the central institutions of the society? In countries where university teachers are civil servants, this question is sometimes settled by the terms of appointment; the teachers have to take an oath to uphold the constitution. This does not, however, mean that a great measure of academic freedom and university autonomy does not exist in such countries. It only means that with the enjoyment of that freedom and that autonomy the university teacher has committed himself to be loyal to the constitution of his society. But these conditions do not obtain in countries in which university teachers are not civil servants. No oaths of loyalty are ordinarily exacted in such circumstances. This does not mean that the university teacher is exempted from the obligation of a minimal loyalty. The obligation is however that of any citizen and not that of a university teacher in particular. The obligation to abstain from subversive activities is the obligation of the citizen, just as is the obligation to abstain from criminal activities. Neither the right to academic freedom nor the autonomy of the university implies any privilege of academics to engage in subversive activities.

The individual owes no more loyalty to his society, its constitution, and its central institutions than does any other citizen and no less. To impose oaths of loyalty on teachers in universities—and other educational institutions—which are not demanded of all other citizens is invidious and unjust. The obligation of respect for the constitution and laws of his society is an obligation which does not derive from his role as a university teacher; it is an obligation inherent in citizenship. Within those limits, the university teacher should be as free as any other free citizen to espouse constitutional changes by constitutional methods.

Academic freedom in the sense of the freedom to perform the academic activities of teaching and research does not confer the freedom of subversion or terrorist activities any more than being a citizen confers such rights in the civil sphere. The autonomy of universities does not confer on individual university teachers immunities which no one else in society legally enjoys.

The autonomy of the university, the academic freedom and the civil freedom of the university teacher together exclude the use of the premises of the university for political purposes. The university teacher is not entitled to use them for any purposes not connected with the performance of his academic obligations of teaching, research, academic administration and academic citizenship. If an academic is active politically, he should not use his office or other university premises for that activity, nor should he use his university address for any correspondence which is part of that activity. (These limitations are not intended to circumscribe the political activities of students which lie beyond the scope of these considerations.)

The university teacher has no obligation to be a conservative, or a liberal, or a social democrat or a radical or a revolutionary. Nor does he have any obligation not to be any one of these. He has, as a university teacher, only the obligations to seek the truth about the subjects he studies and teaches according to the best available methods, to respect and criticise the tradition of his subject and to transmit his knowledge to his students and colleagues with due regard to the criteria of reliability of evidence and of the logical coherence of interpretations and arguments. Some social and political attitudes might be more consistent with the obligations of the university teacher than others but the university teacher as such has no obligation to be consistent if there is a conflict between his academic obligations and the doctrines associated with his political attachment. But as a university teacher his first obligation is to the academic ethic and to what derives from that obligation when he engages in political or publicist activities.

CONCLUDING OBSERVATIONS

The academic ethic is the sum of the obligations which are incumbent upon persons who hold academic appointments. These obligations are derived from the tasks of universities which are to extend and deepen scientific and scholarly knowledge, to educate young and not so young persons in that kind of knowledge and to train them for the practical professions for which that kind of knowledge is required.

The obligations which constitute the academic ethic are not the same as a comprehensive code of conduct for university teachers in all spheres of life. University teachers are many other things as well as university teachers. They are citizens, members of churches, they are parents and spouses. The academic ethic touches only on the acquisition and transmission of scientific and scholarly knowledge within the university and among universities and on activities using that knowledge outside the universities.

Every teacher, whether in kindergarten or graduate school, bears certain moral obligations. Teachers at every level ought not to lie to their pupils, to be cruel to them, whether physically or mentally, ought not to destroy their curiosity, their imagination, their critical powers; they ought, on the other hand, to inform, to train, to develop the capacities of their pupils, to encourage them to face and to overcome their difficulties. These moral responsibilities flow from the very nature of the relationship between pupil and teacher. In dealing with the responsibilities of university teachers we are dealing with a very special class of teachers, working in an institution which is dedicated, which the kindergarten is not, to the advancement of knowledge as well as to its transmission.

In their concern with the advancement of knowledge, university teachers are also not unique in their obligations. A university teacher shares his obligations with the research worker who does his work in research institutes, in industry, or in his own residence—this last is a phenomenon still occasionally encountered in the humanities, if scarcely at all in the physical sciences. Like them, the university teacher engaged in research ought not to falsify his results; like them, he ought to be careful, assiduous, stringent in his criticism of his own work, fair in his criticism of the work done by other scientists and scholars, generous in his acknowledgement of the sources which he has drawn on. But unlike the kindergarten teacher, unlike the persons engaged exclusively in research, the university teacher's obligations arise not only out of his teaching, not only out of his research, but out of the need to conjoin the two within the framework of the university.

Towards the university to which he belongs and which supports him intellectually as well as financially and administratively, the teacher may feel a special loyalty to a degree which varies from time to time, from place to place. Such loyalty reaches its maximum, perhaps, in the fellows of an Oxford or Cambridge college which they help to administer in detail; it reaches its minimum in one of the huge "mass universities" in which the university is thought of, simply, as an institution which provides a living to the practitioners of certain learned professions, their loyalty being more to their professional discipline, and less to the university as such; they conceive of their duties to the university as differing in no vital respect from those of any employee to any employer. In this respect there has been a considerable change of attitude, at least in the Anglo-American world, during the post-war years, as mass universities have come to be the norm, as their administration has fallen more and more into the hands of professional administrators and as, on the other side, science and scholarship have been more and more extensively organised into professional societies, readily linked by rapid communications, so that a "colleague" is as likely to live thousands of miles away as to be a member of the same university. Loyalty to the university, not only to a particular university but to the very idea of a university, has probably diminished, loyalty to the profession has increased. Some of the problems which have beset our universities derive from that very fact.

The university teacher should recall that even in countries where the university teacher is a civil servant or where the attempt is made, by unionisation, to force him into a confrontation of employee and employer, the university is no ordinary place of employment. It is unique in its devotion not to profit-making, not to administration as such, but to learning, in every sense of that word. Often, if by no means invariably, it is an institution which the teacher may be able to modify, or within which he can resist modifications imposed upon it from outside, whether in the name of equality or utility. The university sustains and nourishes the teacher intellectually; it does not simply house him and pay his salary. It is, indeed, an *alma mater*, not only to students but to teachers. Or at least it can be. Its capacity to be an intellectual home for its teachers may be greatly weakened, if those teachers, professionally intent on "getting their own work done", disregard threats to its integrity, whether coming from outside its walls or from within, leaving the care for the university, in a scornful way, to "those who have the time for such things", except when they begin obviously to impinge on their own professional interests—when it is generally far too late to protest.

It is very tempting to think in terms of getting on with the job, to leave concern for one's university to others, until one day the peculiar characteristics of the university, and the job along with it, simply vanish. To act thus is to fail in respect to a special class of moral obligations, obligations towards the university as such.

If the degree to which the teacher can help to shape the future of his university, and of universities generally, varies from institution to institution, from society to society, two things characterise every university everywhere: the university teacher has students and he has colleagues and he has them within the setting of an institution. To his students, to his colleagues and to his institution, the teacher has a variety of obligations but his central obligation is towards the truth. What does this amount to, in concrete terms?

This has been a hard century for the abstract values, not least for truth. Over two thousand years ago, of course, Plato already found it necessary to defend the concept of truth against the Sophists; at the purely philosophical level, the new sceptics are still employing the arguments of their Greek predecessors, Sophists like Protagoras, sceptics like Sextus Empiricus. Yet whatever view we finally take about that still-controverted question of what truth consists in and how it is to be recognised, it takes a hardy sceptic to deny that over the centuries human beings have built up a body of reliable information and that they have done so, in many cases, by those assiduous investigations we call science and scholarship. In the course of such investigations, too, they have developed habits, skills and attitudes of mind which can be passed on to students, who can then employ them to add further to that body of information, whether it be about the physics of the stars, our own bodies or the daily life of ancient Greece.

Even if we ignore the sceptic, as someone who cannot in practice help relying on exactly the same information as the rest of us rely on, two things have certainly to be admitted. The first is that in themselves facts are not necessarily of great interest. With no more developed resources than a telephone book and no more elaborate ability than sheer patience, any of us could construct a vast body of factual truths, relating, let us say, the number of persons in the telephone book whose name begins with "M" to the number of persons who live at an address which contains the number "3". But such truths bear on no problem and are entirely worthless. We would find it hard to rebut the charge that both science and scholarship sometimes present us with some truths which are of scarcely any greater value.

A second point is this: some of the things which even the most conscientious and studious teacher presents to his classes as truths will turn out to be false or at least to need correction. One can exaggerate the extent to which this is so. Most of what we learnt at school still goes unchallenged, even if emphases have changed. Many different views have emerged about the causes and the effects of the French Revolution but the actual account of events remains as it was, unaffected by the varying spotlights which have played upon these events; most of what was taught at school half a century ago in chemistry or mechanics remains unaffected by the great changes which have occurred at the growing points of science since that time. At the university, however, the teacher is operating precisely at those growing points, as part of his function of helping knowledge to advance. The likelihood that what he tells his students will be in need of revision or correction is correspondingly enlarged.

Error, then, the university teacher cannot wholly avoid. But his first obligation is, at the barest minimum, not deliberately to falsify, not to mislead his students, even in the name of some cause to which he attaches great importance. Teachers, not only university teachers, are called upon, in this sense, to have a respect for the truth which admits of no exception. But that is by no means the final extent of the university teacher's obligation to truth. He ought to do what he can to avoid error, however unintentional; that is one reason why he must try to keep abreast of his subject. At all times, there have been university teachers who did not do this, who, even in rapidly changing fields of study, were content to use the same lectures year in and year out. The temptation to act in this way is now greater than it ever was. Pressed to do research, the university teacher may seek out some recondite field, quite remote from his teaching, and excuse the fact that his lectures remain unchanged by pointing to the necessities imposed upon him by his research to concentrate all his reading in that field. Again, the teacher may be simply overwhelmed by the sheer volume of new work. Or he may judge—he has to be careful that this is not an excuse—that the great body of new work is simply a passing fashion which he not only can, but ought to, ignore in his teaching. But whatever the problems which inevitably result, the university teacher has the obligation to ensure that his students are not left with the false impression that what they are being taught represents what is known at a given time, when that is clearly not so.

The situation in this respect will clearly differ from subject to subject. In the case of professional subjects like medicine and engineering, the responsibility is plain; to go on teaching what has been shown to be false is a gross dereliction of duty and a danger to society. In subjects where the conception of knowledge is more uncertain—philosophy, literary theory and the more theoretical reaches of sociology are obvious examples—the teacher is more likely to expound his views, often with very little regard to what is going on elsewhere. And there is no great harm in that, provided that the situation is plain to his students, that it is apparent to them that what he is teaching his students as the truth has been subjected to criticism and to reservations, and which is not unanimously accepted as such. He can do this, for example, by being scrupulous to recommend reading which will make the idiosyncratic bent of his teaching obvious. (There are real problems here; some of the most influential teachers, some of those who are commonly regarded as "great teachers", Wittgenstein, for example, have not done this. But although we are glad to hear from their students what they were taught, we cannot feel that the influence of such teachers on those students was a wholly benign one. In any case, we have to take the ordinary teacher, a respectable scientist or scholar, as our norm, not the very rare genius.)

At a somewhat different level, where we are not concerned with high-level, necessarily controversial, theories but with supposed matters of fact which are nevertheless controversial, the situation is plainer. To take an extreme case: a teacher may be fully convinced that every dissident in the Soviet Union is either insane or in the pay of foreign powers or, on the other side, that there was no holocaust in Nazi Germany. But he ought not to proceed as if these were indisputable facts, of the same order as the date when Lenin entered the Soviet Union or as the original name of Joseph Stalin. He ought not to try to confine the reading of his students to that literature which shares his views; he ought to be prepared to face criticisms. So much, at least, follows from his obligation to the truth.

Of course, there are difficult marginal cases. We, all of us, dismiss certain views as not deserving serious attention. Is the biologist bound to warn his students that there are still creationists or the astronomer that there are still "flat-earthers"? But the general argument is reasonably plain, if not its precise force in marginal, difficult cases: the teacher ought not to pretend that what is controversial is not controversial. Of course, he can still be mistaken. What is apparently settled at one time may be highly controversial at another. The risk of error is part of the human condition. Like everyone else, the university teacher can only do his best to avoid misleading his students. His distinguishing mark lies in the fact that the standards of doing his best are in his case particularly rigorous. And those high standards flow from his special obligations in relation to the truth.

One can light on truths, of course, in many different ways. The university teacher has no monopoly in respect to the discovery of truths. Before he goes to school any child has lit on a great many myths, as a result of his own experience and his communication with his fellows. Not only that, the poet and the sage can light on truths. Then why suppose that the university teacher has distinctive moral obligations arising out of a unique relationship with the truth? In a university such truths, formed by systematically ordered experience and imagination and rational reflection, are brought to the test. Claimants to truth have to make their claims good. The university teacher is dedicated, not only to the truth as such and already established truths but to the spirit of inquiry, curiosity and criticism. Many of his students, to be sure, will never catch that spirit; many will fail to communicate it. Some teachers see themselves, some students see their teachers, simply as purveyors of information, of facts, of unquestionably settled propositions. The greater the degree to which university courses are crammed with facts, as a result of the "knowledge-explosion", the less leisure the student has to think and to work for himself, as a result of the time it takes to cram him with the facts, the less likely it is that this spirit will be communicated and implanted or aroused.

The spirit of inquiry begins from serious problems and tries to solve them within the traditions of science and scholarship. To participate in those traditions one has to be disciplined or trained. More and more, universities take the professions as their model; the scientist and the scholar are anxious to win the support of what they now unselfconsciously refer to as "the profession", a phrase which, not so long ago, would certainly not in the English-speaking world, have been applied to their pursuits by philosophers, scholars and scientists. (The idea of learning as a profession arose in Germany and from there was translated institutionally into the American graduate school.) Two by-products of this idea are the production of much research on trivial problems, in relation to which professional skills can most readily be demonstrated, rather than fundamental problems where the method of proceeding is more uncertain, and passing judgement on what is one in terms of professional standards rather than on its actual intellectual value—as when, let us say, an edition of an important philosopher prides itself on its adherence to professional bibliographical standards and brushes aside the objection that it is going to tell philosphers a great deal that there is no point in thᵥir knowing and will make inaccessible, or wholly ignore, what would really help them. In these circumstances the spirit of inquiry can fly out of the class-room window.

The student disorders of the 1960s were intellectually antinomian; one of the targets of the rebellion was against any sort of training or discipline. The rebellious students were confused, too, in their notions of what constituted "relevance". Yet, in their confused way, some of the students were rebelling against the conception of the university as a place for turning out thoroughly drilled professionals rather than as a place for study and reflection on fundamental problems, arousing intellectual curiosity and assimilating the spirit of inquiry. One of the major problems for the university teacher is to train, without, in the process, narrowing the vision. He has to give expression to a certain kind of deep seriousness, which is not the same thing as solemnity; he must have a "sense of relevance", not as that was understood by those students who meant by it relevance to current social and political issues, but as relevance to those central problems which distinguish an intellectual tradition and which constitute its reason for being.

What the university teacher must not do is to acquiesce in that onslaught on science and scholarship, on disciplined thinking of every kind, so characteristic of the 1960s and still exerting an influence, if now somewhat submerged, beneath a new wave of vocationally minded professionalism. A university teacher who succumbs to that onslaught, who is content to say whatever comes into his mind, without respect for evidence and argument, and who encourages his students to proceed in the same way, is committing the ultimate treason against the university. Systematic, disciplined investigation is its life-blood. Those who reject it as a governing principle have no more place in a university than an atheist has in a church. They are, of course, entitled to attack the universities as an atheist is entitled to attack the churches. But they are lacking in a sense of moral intellectual obligation if they remain within the university, seeking to retain the advantage of membership in it after they have lost faith in the ideals which can alone make sense of it as an institution. The situation of such a university teacher is like that of a priest turned atheist or sceptic and who continues to preach in church. They are both lacking a sense of moral and intellectual obligation. If it is really true that one opinion is as good as another, that there is no such thing as objectivity, then the universities have no function and no justification for their continued existence.

The nature of rational argument, the force of evidence, the extent and character of objectivity—these are topics which can properly be analysed and serious questions may be raised about each of them. Without being sceptical about the value of disciplined inquiry in science and scholarship, one can ask fundamental questions about the way in which it is being conducted and reject as extravagant some of the claims which have been made on its behalf, e.g., the claim that it offers us absolute certainty or the assumption that scientists and scholars are more than human in their ability utterly to cast aside all inherited beliefs or the belief that scientific knowledge alone can provide proper and exhaustive guidance in moral and political decisions. To raise such issues is by no means to be morally irresponsible; nothing can so readily provoke cynicism and scepticism as the making of extravagant claims and the refusal to discuss the postulates of one's position. But such criticisms must themselves, in the context of the university, be propounded and developed in a rationally disciplined way. Moral obligation is rejected only when the teacher is content to make dogmatic pronouncements, to fulminate in a manner which may be perfectly proper in a seer or a prophet, but which has no place in a university.

By developing in his students the capacity to participate in the great traditions of science and scholarship, in however minor a way, by getting them to understand, at the very least, the modes of imagination and the characteristic forms of criticism which they exhibit, a teacher demonstrates his reverence for truth and fulfils the consequential moral obligations, in a manner specific to him as a university teacher. His obligations in relation to truth automatically generate a sense of obligation to his students. If he leaves them with the impression that everything is settled and that there are no longer any but minor problems, or with the belief that when problems were settled in the past it was always either by deduction from dogma or by the application of established methods, then he has failed not only in respect to those students as individuals but in respect to the maintenance of the spirit of inquiry, which is at once rational and reflective. And he is also failing his colleagues in so far as he is neither himself participating in inquiry into fundamental questions nor encouraging his students to do so.

This is connected with the fact that both science and scholarship are collaborative inquiries. Even the most solitary scholar stands, in Newton's famous phrase, on the shoulders of his predecessors. Scientists, natural or social, are far from solitary; they often work as members of teams. Even in the humanities, even in philosophy, the book or article with several authors have become commonplace. This, however, is less important than the collaboration which takes place across the boundaries of research-teams and of single institutions and across the boundaries of countries. Scientists build on the work of other scientists, most frequently outside their own universities and very often in other countries; their publications are read and drawn upon by scientists in other parts of the world. It is approximately similar in the humanistic and social science disciplines, particularly the more abstract ones like linguistics and economics. A scientist or a scholar is a member of an international group with shared assumptions engaged in a common enterprise of exploring a particular class of problems by using particular methods, immediately communicating their results to one another. It is one of a university teacher's responsibilities to arouse and guide his abler students to participation in such groups, disciplining them in the methodical procedures, developing in them the substantive knowledge and the skills and introducing them to the ideals which make collaboration possible. He does not do this by preaching to his students but rather by teaching them with seriousness and devotion and by having some of them participate in his research, as members of his particular group and with some of these becoming, as they move further in their studies, research assistants or junior members of the teaching staff.

What of the ordinary student, not working at a level at which he can expect to be invited to join his teacher's research team? There is a familiar way of referring to universities—as a "community of scholars"—which seems to suggest that every student is automatically a scholar, and some students demand the right to be regarded as such, from the beginning of their university days. But, of course, even the best of them—the rare precocious genius apart—is in fact a learner. A teacher is failing in his obligations if he treats his students as scholars when they are not, if he does not insist that they have to learn. A university, it is more correct to say, is a community of discoverers, teachers and learners. Yet one should not lightly dismiss the feeling which underlies the older designation of the university as a "community of scholars". It suggests that a university teacher should try to do what he can to try to bring home to his students what it is like to be a scholar or a scientist, as distinct from encouraging them to treat some text book as sacred. He will not treat his students as if they were children, even if he cannot treat them as scholars. Otherwise he forgets his obligations to the advancement of knowledge, an advancement which depends in the long run on the sympathetic understanding of a great many persons who are not themselves scientists and scholars but have at least some appreciation of what it is like to be one.

These are the essentials of the academic ethic. There are universities in which it is relatively easy to adhere to it and there are those in which it is more difficult. In universities where there is a tradition of its observance, new members and aspirants among the students who aspire to academic careers, will quite readily assimilate it. There are, however, universities in which the conception of the functions of the institution, promulgated by their higher administrators and accepted by teachers, old and young, is inimical to the academic ethic. Institutions of higher education whose governing members regard them as vocational training schools or as institutions the main task of which is to serve the local community will be less congenial to observance of the academic ethic.

The academic ethos survives through the respect which academics give to their obligations and by the exemplification of it in their own actions before their colleagues, senior and junior, and their students. Students who aspire to academic careers learn the academic ethic by seeing it being practised by their elders. The academic ethic is supported by the conscience of individual academics and their consciousness that their colleagues are adhering to it. Its effective practice by individuals is sustained by the support which it receives in the conduct of colleagues.

Even in the universities in which the academic ethic is best observed, there are many defections and infringements. Quite distinguished scientists and scholars are often self-seeking; some of them are eager to use the power which they exercise in appointments to confer patronage, pay off personal debts or advance the interests of friends and protégés with little consideration for their intellectual and academic merits. Many care only for their own departments, their own special field within their own discipline, and their own conception of the best methods and their own line of substantive interpretation. If it were not so, there would be no need to elaborate and affirm the academic ethic.

The fundamental obligations of university teachers for teaching, research and academic citizenship are the same for all academics. All these activities are necessary for the university to perform its indispensable tasks for modern societies and modern intellectual culture and it falls to the individual academic to contribute up to the best of his capacity to the performance of those tasks. Not all academics are equally endowed or equally inclined, for whatever reason, to the activities needed to meet these obligations. Some are much more inclined and much better endowed for research, others more clearly for teaching and some are better equipped for academic citizenship than others. Nevertheless, to abstain from any of these totally and to show no respect for them is contrary to the obligations of an academic career.